Mariachi
for
Gringos

Unlocking the Secrets
of
Mexico's Macho Music

More praise for *Mariachi for Gringos*...

"Immensely readable, but even more usable. This collection of all-you-need-to-know about mariachi, whether you're a 'gringo' or not, is indispensable to anyone interested in having a great time when you are *anywhere* that this infectious music is being performed."

-Christina Tostado, Special Projects Buyer, Bowers Museum, Huntington Beach, CA

"Wow! This take-along little volume proves, once again, that great works often come in small packages. This is all you need to progress from a neophyte to an aficionado in one enjoyable evening."

-Joy DuRae Eicher, U.S. Government Teacher, Battle Creek, MI

"Gracias, amigo! My husband and I have always enjoyed listening (and dancing) to mariachi songs. Now we appreciate them so much more after reading this book. It is a valuable gem for everyone."

-Helena Sabala, Principal, Valle Lindo Elementary School, Chula Vista, CA

"...An eye (and an ear) opener for all 'gringos' and not-so-gringos. Great research, logically arranged... proving that it can still be fun to learn. It certainly helped me understand a vital part of my culture as I sang along with the songs included... Only mariachi music gives you this rush!"

-Enrique Villalvazo, Attorney-At-Law, Tijuana, Baja California, México

"A great resource... enlightening, wonderfully researched, a brilliant pocket companion for travelers, musicians, scholars, 'everyman' (and every woman)... very informative."

-James Elliott Easley, Director of Music, Tiffany School, Eastlake, CA

"This book gets you in tune with the music of Mexico and gives a real appreciation for its authenticity and traditions. It's a great read and an even better pocket pal."

-Sherrie Strausfogel, author of "Hawaii's Spa Experience: Rejuvenating Secrets of Islands," as well as contributor to nine Gault-Millau 'Guides to Southern California', Honolulu, HI

"Thoroughly enjoyable...both informative and easy to read. Although I grew up in a traditional Mexican home, I still had many unanswered questions about this music. I would recommend this volume to anyone wanting to learn more about mariachi that is now being performed internationally, even up here in 'The last Frontier.'"

-Adam Galindo, Jr., Vice President, Taco Loco Products, Anchorage, AK

"The Spanish conquistadores never found the mythical cities of gold. Instead, they accidentally co-created the golden age of Mariachi-a musical tradition flowing out of the soul of Jalisco that ran as deep and rich as the silver mines of Taxco. The author expertly weaves the threads of language, history, and music that make up this rich tapestry."

-Jerome Kocher, World History Teacher, Sweetwater High School, National City, CA

Mariachi
for
Gringos

Unlocking the Secrets
of
Mexico's Macho Music

Gil Sperry

Amigo del Mar Press
San Diego

Amigo del Mar Press

PO Box 439060
San Diego, CA 92143-9060

Front Cover Art: Denise Sperry's "Locked Up," a watercolor rendition of the Ensenada (Baja California, Mexico) Military Garrison's original solitary confinement cell door. Used with the express permission of the artist.

Rear Cover Art: Bryan Relyea's "Latina Mariachera," a mural created for Masa Restaurant in Minneapolis, Minnesota. Used with the express permission of D'Amico and Partners.

Library of Congress Cataloging-in-Publication Data

Sperry, Gil.
   Mariachi for Gringos: Unlocking the Secrets of Mexico's
Macho Music / Gil Sperry p. cm.
Includes bibliographical references.
ISBN-13: 978-1-4243-0316-8
ISBN-10: 1-4243-0316-8
      1.   Music 2. Mexico 3. Mariachi I. Title

   2006904741

Printed in the United States of America

First Edition, 2006
Second Edition, 2007

Dedication

This book is dedicated to the memory of my dear son, Matthew, a gentle soul, a protean and incredibly talented professional musician who fit no mold except that of loving husband and father. He was taken from us in 2003 when he was struck by a truck while riding his bicycle to his "day job" at LeapFrog in Berkeley, California, where he was writing music for software used to help young children fall deeper in love with music.

He and his contributions are forever remembered by his family, including his wife, Stacia and his daughter, Lila, as well as his extended "family of friends" around the world.

My wife, Priscilla, and I will never forget the last night we spent with him at his home in Oakland. He had sent me two wonderful CDs that he'd recorded with great *mariachi* musicians in Jalisco, Mexico. I told him that night that he was "my role model." His greatest wish was for a world at peace, and I pray that we will all make the effort to make that wish come true.

"The only thing more Mexican than *tequila* is *mariachi* and it seems a shame to have one without the other."

Camille Collins, *What is Mariachi?*

"When a song is a standard, it can reproduce itself from one of its constituent parts. If you recite the words, you will hear the melody. Hum the melody and the words will form in your mind…Nothing else can as suddenly and poignantly evoke the look, the feel, the smell of our times past."

E. L. Doctorow, *City of God*

Contents

Acknowledgements

I would like to offer my utmost gratitude to the *maestra* herself, Laura Sobrino. Without her tireless efforts on my behalf, this volume would never have been completed. That she found the time to help in spite of her incredibly busy teaching, performing, arranging and publishing schedule is not an inconsiderable *milagrito*.

In addition, she found the time to contact many others on my behalf, including: Hector Aguiniga, Antonio Briseño, Frank & Jennifer Candelaria, Richard Carranza, Randy Carrillo, Cynthia Chio, Jon Clark, Danielle Correa, Antonio Covarrubias, Dinorah Curkendall, Lucero Delgado, Barbara Diaz, Alberto Estrada, Mark Fogelquist, Desiree Garcia, Frank Gil, Angelica Gomez, Jesus Gonzalez, Frank Grivalva, Juan Manuel Hernandez, Betty Herrera, Jimmy Leger, Celia Leyva, Eric Long, George Lopez, Debra Martinez, Jay Melendez, Israel Molina, Norma Monteza, Juan Morales, Fernando Moreno, Nancy Muñoz, Jeff Nevin, Marisa Orduño, Mima Orozco, Griselda Perez, Leonor Perez, M. E. Perez, Kristine Penner, Jim Petty, Elena Robles, Rodri Rodriguez, Russell Rodriguez, Nydia Rojas, Junko Seki, Dan Sheehy, Henry Spiller, Megan Starks, Adrian Vaca, Al Valverde, Sally Vega, and John Vela. My thanks to all.

To my editor, the indefatigable Robert Schoen, a consummate musician and published author in his own right (as well as a passionate advocate for this book), I'll never be able to adequately express my gratitude. The many weeks (and late nights) he spent counseling and cajoling me until the project was completed are so appreciated.

Others that helped to make the dream become reality include authors John Kenny Crane (Dean Emeritus of San Jose State University) and Beverley Crane. Jerome Kocher used his extensive graphic arts experience to produce covers that perfectly captured the essence of the project. Denise Sperry, whose award-winning watercolor "Locked Up" was the inspiration for the book's subtitle, offered artistic suggestions that became significant additions. Cookie Valenzuela gave invaluable help with idiomatic translations from Spanish to English, and Olga Peña and Christina Tostado assisted in hunting down obscure source materials.

Finally, all my love to my wife, Priscilla, for putting up with my usual idiosyncrasies during the prolonged period it took to complete this book, very much a "labor of love."

I hope you enjoy reading and using *Mariachi for Gringos* as much as I enjoyed writing it.

Gil Sperry

Baja California

Preface

One sultry summer evening in July 1975, my wife and I were on vacation in tropical *Puerto Vallarta*. We had not been successful in our hunt for an air-conditioned restaurant on the beach; but we did find a very popular spot called "Moby Dick" that featured both fresh seafood, courtesy of the *Bahia Banderas*, and fresh breezes, courtesy of some rapidly whirling ceiling fans. We made yet another "find" on that very pleasant evening, the music called *mariachi*. When the nine musicians, clad in matching black and silver outfits, complete with embroidered *sombreros*, made their way to our table, we had no idea what to expect. Short on Spanish, as well as ignorant of the proper protocol, we were very definitely two bewildered *gringos*. We recognized some of the instruments that the musicians were holding— a guitar, two trumpets, and four violins. Others, including a convex-backed five stringed cousin to the guitar and a six stringed bigger brother, definitely related to a double bass, were totally unfamiliar to us. We later found out that they were called, respectively, the *vihuela* and *guitarrón*. When we just shrugged our shoulders and turned our hands palms-up at the question asked by the band's obvious leader, the group immediately burst into song…and *mariachi*, Mexico's home-grown music, had given birth to two more life-long fans.

Looking back on that evening, I realize that we really knew very little about what we were enjoying. First, we had no knowledge of the history of *mariachi*—the name given not only to the music but to the group and its individual members, as well. We also had no idea about the protocol to follow when the musicians approached our table. For example, do we eat while they play? And, finally, we had no idea what the lyrics meant (what was the story that the song was telling?).

Many years later, I'm more certain than ever that most English-speaking visitors to Mexico still need help in these three areas. For that reason, I compiled *Mariachi for Gringos*. You will find the history and proper protocol for becoming an informed *mariachi aficionado,* as well as 50 of the most requested *mariachi* standards. The music for these classics includes annotated melody lines and chords, as well as the Spanish lyrics and English translations. Best of all, everything is in a format designed to fit into your jeans, back (or fanny) pack, or purse. Take it along with you on your next trip to anywhere *mariachi* is played, including many Mexican restaurants and *cantinas* in the U.S.A., and begin to enjoy your experience to the fullest.

Mariachi "Pop-Quiz"

This short quiz will give you an idea of just how much there is to know about *mariachi*. Circle the choices before continuing. Then when you finish reading the next section (The History of *Mariachi)*, you can test yourself to see how much you have really learned. I'm sure you'll find some surprises as a more comprehensive knowledge of *mariachi* history triumphs over your preconceptions.

Mariachi is:

A. Mexican folk music.

B. An individual musician who plays Mexican folk music.

C. A group of musicians who play Mexican folk music from a notated arrangement.

D. The French word for marriage (*mariage*).

E. A festival to honor a virgin known as *Maria H* (Maria AH-chay).

F. The *Coca* Indian word for "musician."

G. The *Coca* word for "wood."

H. The *Coca* pre-Hispanic five-tone system of music notation.

I. The combination of the *Coca* five-tone system and the European twelve-tone system, which was brought to the New World by the Spanish in 1519.

J. Played exclusively by men.

K. The only music that features the *vihuela* and the *guitarrón*.

L. The sound exemplified by Herb Alpert and the Tijuana Brass

M. An amalgam of Indian, Spanish, and African musical influences.

The History of *Mariachi*

Early History and The Coca

In the early 1500s, the *Coca* tribe of what is today central Jalisco had already developed a relatively sophisticated system of rhythmic music played primarily at their religious celebrations. They had created primitive instruments including rattles, drums, reeds carved from the trees of their prolific forests, flutes baked from the plentiful red clay, and conch-shell horns from the sea. Their music employed combinations of five tones created, in part, by varying the thickness of the drum walls and the tautness of the animal skins stretched over them and by covering different combinations of the small holes in the wind instruments while the player blew through a larger hole at one end.

Although the *Coca* language is now extinct, most current experts believe that they used the word *mariachi* to describe the musicians among them. A few of the experts believe that *mariachi* was what the Indians called their source of wood, the *pillo* and *cirima* trees.

In any event, prior to the arrival of the Spanish (with their "treasure" of the European twelve-tone system and some very interesting new instruments), it would probably be accurate to say that the *Coca* people were a rhythm section in search of melody lines.

In 1519, **Hernán Cortés** landed in Mexico. On board his eleven ships were soldiers, implements of war (including horses) and men of the cloth. When his fighting men became unhappy with the austerity of their new home, many expressed a desire to return to Spain. Cortés dealt with this dissent by emptying the ships of all men and supplies, sailing the vessels to a highly visible location just off shore, setting fire to all but the one he was on and sinking the other ten as his dissatisfied warriors watched. Cortés then announced the results of the vote recount: a unanimous "landslide" in favor of staying and completing their mission to conquer the New World.

The Franciscan friars who were part of this expeditionary force brought not only the European twelve-tone system of music and three unique stringed voicings, but the liturgy of the Catholic Church as well. This combination proved irresistible to the *Coca*. It was necessary for them to learn the Spanish language so as to read the music, understand the lyrics, and become proficient on these new instruments. The *padres* were only too happy to teach them all they could, especially since it led directly to their ultimate goal of converting the natives to Catholicism. The twelve-tone system, of course, has survived until the present and is still used in all but the most avant-garde Western music.

The Spaniards introduced the *Coca* to the harp, the *vihuela*, and the *guitarra*. The harp, although large and unwieldy, had the initial musical advantage of versatility. It could function as a bass line, a chordal accompaniment, or as a melody line. The *vihuela*, convex-backed, highly portable, and five-stringed, served primarily as a melody line. Its rich, resonant timbre was, apparently, much admired by the *Coca*, for it has outlasted the harp as part of the amalgam of the indigenous and Hispanic music that evolved. The *guitarra* (its full name was the *guitarra de golpe*) was a bit smaller than the modern guitar and was used initially as a rhythm instrument.

The earliest reliable eye witness account describing the relationship between the *Coca* and the Spanish comes from a Franciscan monk, **Brother Miguel de Bolonia**. In 1532, he arrived in *Cocula,* the home of the *Coca,* and supervised the building of a

4

church. The Franciscans taught the Indians how to read, write, and count in Spanish, to play instruments, to read music, and to learn the musical portion of the Catholic Church services. The mixture of the new and the old instruments, music, and lyrics led the *Coca* to use one of their "lost words" (from the language spoken at their former home city that had been destroyed by a mammoth waterspout) to describe their musicians. That word was *mariachi*, *Coca* for "music group." This is the first use of the word, *mariachi*, that can be verified.

How was the word *mariachi* created ? This word is formed from three distinct parts: *mari, ia,* and *chi*. *Mari* originally was the *Coca* word for "deer," as well as a synonym for the deer's ability "to run fast." *Ia* meant "the sound," while *chi* meant "what." "What sounds in a fast speed" was how the *Coca* described their ability to play music at an extreme up-tempo, "deer-like" velocity. In addition, *mariachi* had two other meanings: "tree" and/or "a wooden platform on which to dance."

De Bolonia reports that, shortly thereafter, the *Coca* founded a new community that would exclusively focus on teaching and performing the melded music. The village was called *Guitarilla* after a new instrument the locals created, modeled after the *guitarra de golpe*. The *guitarilla* was smaller and had only four strings. Although influenced by the Spanish, the *Coca mariachi* started their music academy in the mountains of what is today the modern Mexican state of *Jalisco*, as far away from a continuing European influence as they could get. This isolation led to the creation of a music that was unlike that of any other regions, closer to (and thus more closely influenced by) the Spanish. As the musical *Coca* moved to higher ground, the word *mariachi* had evolved into meaning "the sounds from the hilltop."

5

Check Your Answers

Returning to our quiz, we seem to have proven that answers F and G are historically correct. And thus, it's apparent that the word *mariachi* did *not* come from the French word for marriage (*mariage*) or the music played at wedding celebrations during **Emperor Maximillian's** occupation of Mexico (1862-1867). In fact, this early theory was thoroughly debunked in 1991 with the discovery of a series of communications between a local priest, **Cosme Santa Anna**, and his bishop dating from 1852, ten years before the French "connection," that discusses *mariachi* and their music. Answer D, therefore, is not correct. And while we are debunking, we might as well address another specious story, that the word comes from an annual festival in honor of a virgin named Maria *H.*(pronounced in Spanish as Maria AH-chay) at which musicians played who were, over time, given the collective name of *mariachi*. The *Coca* far predated this later-day Catholic holiday. Answer E is also incorrect.

Although it appears obvious that the music of both the Europeans and the native Indians had begun to mix, there are those who claim that there is no linkage between what these two groups had created and the *mariachi* we hear today. To complicate matters even more, a third type of music was introduced into the blend when African slaves were brought to Mexico in the 17th century. What occurred, over time, was a new music called *mestizo* (mixed). Did this musical melting pot evolve into modern *mariachi*? Can we ever be sure? Probably not. But, if we agree that we are influenced by what comes before us, can there be any doubt that what we have today was influenced by what we had then. A five-tone system of *Coca* music (and its primitive instruments) was joined with a twelve-tone system of European music (and its more sophisticated instruments). These were then combined

6

with a third music (with different instruments) brought from Africa. Did modern *mariachi* develop in a vacuum or was it inexorably driven to where it is today by what it was yesterday? Common sense and the test of time both support the latter position; answers H, I, and M, therefore, appear correct as well.

The 17th and 18th Centuries

For most of the remainder of the 17th (and well into the 18th) century, the musical stew of *mestizo* continued to cook. It was, without a doubt, the dominant form of Mexican folk music. Its evolution was marked by the movement of the country's finest practitioners of the art to an area west of Guadalajara, in the state of Jalisco. These musicians were still, collectively, known as *mariachi*. Historical references discuss the use of other instruments, perhaps African in origin. One was called the *caja* (or box drum). However, most of the contemporary illustrations and supporting written histories of this period (and into the 19th century), unequivocally point to the predominant use of stringed instruments in *mariachi*.

How had the instrumentation, although still primarily stringed, changed since the early 16th century arrival of the Spanish? Initially, the *cuarteto mariachi* group included the harp, the *guitarra de golpe*, and two violins. Although the 3/4- size guitar variant survived, the large size and relative awkwardness of the harp contributed to that instrument's gradual decline in use. The more easily carried bass line instrument, the *guitarrón,* soon replaced the ponderous harp. The melody lines were assigned to the violins, while the *vihuela* had evolved from a melodic instrument into one providing an harmonic and rhythmic accompaniment. It is interesting to note the uniqueness of these two additions to the *mariachi* line-up. No other type of music employs the five (treble) stringed *vihuela* or its six (bass) stringed convex bellied "big brother," the *guitarrón*. So, if you chose YES on K, you were correct.

Mariachi Evolves

The evolution of where the music was commonly played is also quite interesting. It had become the centerpiece in multiple day celebrations, where everybody ate, drank, and danced to excess. These parties, primitive Woodstocks, if you will, often resulted in injuries and illnesses for the participants. Contrast this "popular" *mariachi* to the "purist" *mariachi* of the Guadalajara area where the descendants of the *Coca* brought the music to ever-higher levels of excellence. Wherever these *maestros* played, the music itself was the primary attraction. In pursuit of an even more authentic sound, they used only stringed instruments that they had constructed themselves: violins, *vihuelas ,*and *guitarrónes* built from local white wood with strings made from dried cat or skunk intestines.

Another interesting evolutionary direction concerns itself with the content of what the musicians played. Originally, we know that the spiritual side of life was their major concern, both before and after the arrival of the Spaniards. But when the *Coca* headed for the hills, the strong influence of secular life soon became the prevailing factor. After the discovery that their up-tempo rhythms lent themselves to oft requested dance tunes, the musicians decided to diversify and use their music for an ever-widening variety of purposes. The *criollos* (Mexicans of Spanish descent) wrote popular music, often critical of Spain in a satirical way that was considered irreverent by the conquerors. Some of the tunes also had ribald lyrics that did very little to mollify the Spanish. From religious music to dance tunes, the *mariachi* had now begun to take on a politically sensitive, anti-clerical, and scandalous edge. The best way for them to express this new myriad of meanings was to create different types of music for each. This fractionalization was a major factor in *mariachi* becoming Mexico's national music

Types of Mariachi

Let us take a moment now to examine this dichotomy since the songs you request on your next night out at a Mexican restaurant or cantina, whether in the *Estados Unidos* (United States) or Mexico, are more than just interesting melodies.

The consensus of most historians of *mariachi* is that the original music was dance oriented. The first short dance tunes were called *jarabes*. In the early 1700s, innovative musicians began to weave "strings" of *jarabes* into longer selections which they called *sones*. The *sones* soon began to incorporate satirical lyrics, most often aimed at the pomposity of church and state. Additional topics for the *sones* included all aspects of rural life. Many *sones* had one of two purposes. One group of tunes was purely bucolic in nature, describing flora and fauna. The second group concerned itself with people and their foibles. In pursuit of a wider audience for *sones*, the lyrics were often controversial in their comparisons of the mating rituals of barnyard animals with the actions of the people who tended them. Courtship was a popular topic for *sones*.

Sones are a keystone of *mariachi* music. Besides their frequently provocative story lines, they have several easily recognizable musical traits. Their very danceable rhythms usually alternate between 3/4 waltz time and 6/8, with strong, syncopated beats. Some of the most popular *sones* include *Guadalajara* (the name of the capital city of what is today the state of Jalisco) and *La Bamba* (the name of the type of dance, like mambo or rumba). But putting meaningful lyrics aside, it is essential to note that, first and foremost, *mariachi* music was meant for dancing. The *jarabe,* essentially a medley of dance pieces that might include polkas, for instance, was still the overriding reason for the popularity of *mariachi.* Arguably, the single most recognizable melody of the genre is the famous *Jarabe Tapatio* (*jarabe* means dance, *tapatio* is the nickname for a resident of Guadalajara). It is often the centerpiece of the performances of many national Folkloric dance troupes. While it is true that it is mostly associated with Guadalajara, the capital city of Jalisco and the cradle of *mariachi*, this song is almost universally known today as *The Mexican Hat Dance.*

The entire idiom of dance tunes became a showpiece tradition based on the Spanish *flamenco.* The Mexicans called their adaptation *zapateado.* The dancers energetically drove the heels of their *zapatas* (shoes) into the wooden dance floor, their rhythmic, high volume tapping complementing the music accompanying them.

Most electrifying of all was the performance called *huapango* where the couples lined up in opposing columns on the wood platform dance floors. The men usually wore the traditional *vaquero* (cowboy) garb while the women were decked out in *rebozos* (shawls) and sequins. The dancers' upper bodies remained perfectly erect while their feet performed a feat of biped magic; in some instances, glasses of water were balanced on the dancers' heads to more clearly draw attention to the disparity between what their torsos were not doing and what their toes were!

With all the emphasis on the dance, *sones* continued to grow in importance and not only in Jalisco. *Sones* from the birthplace became known as *sones jalisciences.* Their popularity also grew in Veracruz, where they became known as either *sones veracruzano* or *sones jarochos, La Bamba* being the most famous example. In the *huasteca,* a region north of Veracruz, they were called *sones huastecos* or *huapangos.* A singer of *huapangos* was called a *huapangero;* this style of singing was often characterized by high-pitched falsetto breaks. Interestingly enough, even at this early date, there was evidence of *mariachi* becoming Mexico's national music. *Sones* were commonly performed in all three regions and thus had to have sprung from common melodic roots.

For two very different reasons, the evolution from *jarabes* (dances) to *sones* (songs) took a sharp turn at the end of the 18ᵗʰ century when melodies with much slower tempos were introduced. The first was probably to give the hardworking musicians a break, since playing a continuous, lengthy set of up-tempo numbers was physically taxing on the performers (and on the dancers). The second, at least equally as important, was the introduction of romance (the serious side of courtship) into the *mariachi* repertoire. Sensual *serenatas* (serenades) and *boleros* (songs of passion) became the acceptable method for a man to send an expression of love to his girlfriend during a time when physically separating young members of the opposite sex was of paramount importance to both sets of parents. Excellent examples of this music with meaningful messages include *Por un Amor (For a Love)* and *Sabor a Mi (The Taste of Me)*. In less than a century, *mariachi* had taken a significant series of steps from the barnyard to the bedroom.

Canciones and *corridas* (songs with stories to be sung) were closely related to *serenatas* and *boleros*. Several songs of this expanded genre are among the most beloved in the *mariachi* repertoire. Primary examples include *Cuando Calienta El Sol (When The Sun Is Hot), Cielito Lindo (The Beautiful Sky), Las Mañanitas (The Early Morning,* a popular song for birthday celebrations), and *Cucurrucucu Paloma (The Cooing Of The Dove).*

Rancheras (songs evocative of life on the ranch) also became very popular. Interestingly, the clothing worn by the itinerant musicians playing this type of *vaquero* (cowboy) refrain seemed to improve as their economic expectations rose. The early practitioners of *mariachi* initially wore the "uniform" of the Jalisco peasant class: white cotton pants, matching shirts, and leather sandals. Their costumes changed to what the typical *hacienda* owners wore (the *traje de charro*: black and silver with matching embroidered *sombreros*), as these wealthy *dons* became the role models to which the *mariachi* aspired. The music of ranch life became uplifting, as well. Several classic *rancheras* include *El Rey (The King), El Rancho Grande (The Big Ranch), Ella (She),* and *Volver, Volver (Return, Return).*

By the 19th century it would be accurate to describe the music that had evolved as multifaceted. The lyrics spoke of such diverse themes as love, hatred, betrayal, *machismo*, death, religion, politics, heroes, villains, animals, and even insects—*La Cucaracha (The Cockroach)*. But, unlike the music that developed in Europe during the same period, Mexico could not point to a Mozart or Beethoven as a driving force behind its indigenous musical art form.

There were at least two major reasons for this lack of a central coalescing force. First, until this time, the music had remained a potpourri of influences, owing whatever cohesiveness it had to a largely rural-based population of practitioners. They were predominantly peasants and always peripatetic. Attired in the garb of the common workingman, they attempted to earn more than a laborer's wage by seeking pay for providing musical services to distant *haciendas*. When they found the employment they were looking for, they ceased their seemingly endless travels, but when this happened, the spread of their music ceased as well.

Secondly, musicians were not only isolated by geography but just as importantly, if not more so, by the lack of a written, annotated method of spreading their music to other regions. Fear of having their creations plagiarized by others must have played a part, too. All the music and lyrics were learned by listening and then memorizing what was heard. For nearly 200 years, songs had been passed down from father to son, from generation to generation, solely by ear. The professionalism of a *mariachi* was measured by how many songs he had learned in this manner. The size of his repertoire was also a measure of his earning capacity.

While employed at the far-flung *haciendas*, the *mariachi* provided the musical centerpiece for every social occasion: baptisms, confirmations, weddings, anniversaries, holy days, *fiestas* and funerals. Request lists from the recently departed were many times given to the musicians: these tunes were usually played following the formal service. Some of the all-purpose powerhouse groups became known through word-of-mouth far outside of their geographic spheres of influence. One of them from Tecalitlán was founded in 1850 by **Amado Vargas**, a local musician of great repute. Many mark this as the beginning of the golden age of modern *mariachi* as Vargas' son, **Gaspar**, and his grandson, **Silvestre**, would become the acknowledged masters of the music in the years to come. In 1905, *mariachi* got another huge boost in prestige when a group directed by **Justo Villa** was invited to play at

13

the Mexico City inauguration of President **Porfirio Diaz**, as well as at the patriotic celebrations that followed. The capital's populace fell in love with the bright, upbeat music, which seemed to flow effortlessly from the traditional *mariachi* strings. The players' peasant garb added to the illusion of one nation united. Shortly thereafter, the Revolution of 1910 shattered that illusion.

The 1900s

During the revolution (1910 to 1917) the *mariachi* were now forced to leave their secure bases at the haciendas and once again became itinerant. They traveled to the cities where they attempted to earn a living by playing songs for fees at public venues, singing of revolutionary heroes whenever possible. New types of songs and dances had to be added to appeal to the more sophisticated urban, pro-nationalistic audiences. This new patriotic music soon became widespread in its popularity. The best of the old days was combined with the current heroism and the country's hopes for the future. The spirit of *mariachi* became every bit as important to the people of Mexico during these crucial seven years, just as the image of the trio of wounded drummer, flautist, and flag bearer had been to the residents of the original Thirteen American Colonies in 1775.

Those who had fought for and seemingly won freedom would never forget *mariachi*. Since the inauguration of President **Alvaro Obregón** in 1920, every Mexican president, including **Felipe Calderón**, has employed *mariachi* music as a key indicator of his concern for Mexico's rank-and-file. As the popularity of *mariachi* has grown and the socio-economic status of its musicians has improved, the typical group's size, instrumentation, appearance, sound and repertoire has also kept pace.

The Musicians and Their Instruments

At the turn of the century, the typical *mariachi* group consisted of four musicians. Two violins, a *vihuela* and a *guitarrón* were the standard instrumentation with everyone sharing in the vocals. The first addition to this lineup came shortly after 1920 with a wind instrument being incorporated into the previously all-string ensemble. The cornet was the initial addition, although the trumpet soon replaced it. No one is entirely sure how or why the *pistón* (cornet) came to be the first non-stringed instrument in *mariachi*, but there is an interesting time-honored anecdote that is worth sharing.

One day a poor cornetist named Jesús arrived in Cocula (ancestral home of the *Coca*). He begged his only friends in the town, members of a *mariachi* group, to allow him to play with their band. Their response was a resounding "no" because the cornet was not considered suitable for the *mariachi* sound. The director of the group, however, felt sorry for the down-and-out player. He invited Jesús to live with him and his family for a while until he had gathered enough resources to move on to a place of his own. Jesús accepted the director's very kind offer and was even allowed to observe the *mariachi* as they practiced. The enterprising visitor began to memorize the tunes that the group played and then, out of earshot of its members, began to practice all of the melodies on his cornet until he had mastered them. The group was hesitant at first when they heard Jesus play their songs, but they allowed him to sit in with them, as long as he used a mute so that the horn's sound would not overpower the other instruments. Gradually, the director and the rest of the players began to like the effect and decided to let Jesus play a couple of numbers with them at their next performance as long as he would continue to use his mute. Imagine everyone's surprise when the audience applauded the cornet's inclusion and enthusiastically asked for it to be included in everything the group was going to play. Truth or fiction, we're not certain, but we do know that the larger, louder trumpet, which became a requisite component of contemporary *mariachi*, soon replaced the cornet.

Following the apocryphal tale of the boy and his horn, the story of how the *trompeta* (trumpet) was inserted into *mariachi* seems to have a firmer basis in fact. In the mid-1920s, **Emilio Azcaraga,** the founder of Mexico City's first radio station, XEW, was in desperate search of an instrumental voice for *mariachi* that was more powerful and of a higher pitch. This voicing was necessary due to the intermittent static that plagued his station's musical broadcasts.

After the trumpet, the next instrument that was added to *mariachi* was the Spanish guitar. Predictably, it was another melody voicing to counteract the over-riding fear of the brass wind instrument overpowering the traditionally predominant silky sound of the strings. The Spanish guitar (also called the *guitarra cesta*) was slightly wider than the classical guitar and also a bit deeper in tone. It provided a balance between the upper register resonance of the *vihuela* and the big bass backbeat of the *guitarrón*, as well as a melodic counterbalance to the trumpet. Proponents of the "new" bold, brassy, trumpet sound countered by adding another horn.

The ante was then raised again by the "string-o-philes" who trumped with one, two, and sometimes even three additional violins. *Ad infinitum, ad absurdum*? Not really, since the greater number of instruments led to increasingly rich musical overlays of melody, harmony, and rhythm. Today, there are *mariachi* groups consisting of three or more trumpets, six to eight violins, a Spanish guitar, a *vihuela*, and a *guitarrón*. Some groups have even added novelty instruments like the flute, the accordion (arriving with an influx of German settlers into northern Mexico) and, in a return engagement, the Mexican folk harp. However, these last three are the exception rather than the rule and have not been accepted as part of the mainstream *mariachi* instrumentation.

As the *mariachi* increasingly moved to the city in search of a more rewarding life and their music became more sophisticated, they found venues that specifically brought their audiences to them. One of the first and, still today, one of the most famous, was the **Plaza Garibaldi** in Mexico City. In 1923, a *cantina* called the **Salon Tenampa** opened on what is today the *plaza* and immediately became known as the place to be to hear the most popular *mariachi* in the region. Groups wishing to achieve national recognition traveled from all over Mexico to this centralized location.

An early day "battle of the bands" ensued on a regular basis and each competitor had its loyal base of fans. Interestingly enough, the music was the sole differentiating factor; the uniform of the day for all but the very poorest of the newcomers was the *traje de charro* (suit of the horseman). And it is noteworthy that this outfit has not undergone much change in the years since. The players, then and now, were often clad in *chalecos* (waist length jackets) over *monos* (bow ties), a wide *cinturon* (belt), *pantalones* (tightly fitted wool pants with no back pockets) that were flared at the ankles to accommodate *botines* (short cowboy boots), and *sombreros* (wide brimmed hats). The color of choice, as on the *haciendas* decades before, was black. The ornamentation could be embroidery, leather appliqués, or usually *botanaduras* (silver buttons).

Another major factor in the 1920s that led to the growth of *mariachi*'s popularity was the invention of the radio. Now, for the very first time, the entire country, not just those on *haciendas* or in selected metropolitan locations, could listen to this national music. Repertoires grew as the nation's appetite for new songs with deep meaning became insatiable. The unique sound of *mariachi* was once described as "...a musical *serape* (blanket) of many wildly contrasting wide bands of aural colors appearing side-by-side." Smooth-as-silk violins, vibrant trumpets, the bass heartbeat of the *guitarrón*, the resonant, high-pitched *vihuela*, combined with the complementary Spanish guitar, all blending and contrasting with harmonizing voices telling provocative stories. The combination was irresistible.

As the demands on the size, instrumentation, appearance, sound, and repertoire of *mariachi* grew, the need for an innovator to take the music to the next level was readily apparent. And, as so often happens, forces had already been set in motion that would create the correct environment for this innovator to emerge. In 1930, the stewardship of the famous group **Mariachi Vargas de Tecalitlán** had passed to its third generation leader, Silvestre Vargas. He has since been recognized as "...the greatest *mariachi* organizer and visionary of all time." In 1934, he permanently moved the group to Mexico City, recognizing correctly that this was the center of the *mariachi* universe and would remain so for the foreseeable future. After being asked to play for the inauguration of the wildly popular President **Lázaro Cárdenas** in that very same year, all of the country's finest *mariachi* who heard the band's incredibly inspiring performance aspired to play for Vargas. President Cárdenas fueled these flames with his passion for furthering all aspects of Mexico's culture that were unique.

Realizing his own shortcomings, perhaps the surest sign of a genuine visionary, Silvestre Vargas hired a professionally trained musician, **Rubén Fuentes**, as his Musical Director. Fuentes was also a talented *mariachi* in his own right. A classically educated musician's mind and a *mariachi*'s heart united in one person for the very first time would prove to be the breakthrough combination. Fuentes, with Vargas' approval and assistance, wrote sparkling arrangements for many of the traditional *sones*. Together they composed new *sones* and *huapangos*; they also produced arrangements for many of the top singers and songwriters of their era. These famous names in the Spanish-speaking world included **Pedro Infante, Miguel Aceves Mejia, Lola Beltran** and **Jose Alfredo Jiminez,** better known as the creator of exemplary *rancheros* and *boleros*. See the section "Famous Mariachi Songs and Their Composers." It became readily apparent that the musicians of Mariachi Vargas would have had to be able to read music if they were to be able to play Fuentes' arrangements. The "old" way of the aural tradition, learning songs and techniques by listening, was no longer acceptable. The time-honored methods of several centuries would no longer suffice. Vargas and Fuentes were writing a new definition of professionalism. Only complete musicians were acceptable. The modern *mariachi* was now being asked to read music, play by ear, sing, transpose, improvise, and when requested, to play unfamiliar songs at a professional level.

The introduction of radio was only the first step in the growth of *mariachi*. Recorded music, late in coming to Mexico, was next and, finally, in the 1930s, the introduction of motion pictures with sound. Many who found the music of Mariachi Vargas pleasing, first bought their recordings and then went to see many of the 200 films that they appeared in and scored over the next decade. Films made in Mexico for the national audience grew in popularity, and *mariachi* was a major factor in the formula for success. The members of the Vargas troupe became the pride of Ciudad de México and major international celebrities as well, as they developed a huge following in other parts of the Hispanic world. They were the "strolling orchestra/

19

choir" ideal to which all other instrumental/vocal combination groups aspired. In Mexico, they were the kings of the *mariachi* world; it was impossible to overestimate their importance and influence. Their two trumpet harmonies, combined with multiple violins, were the standard instrumentation for any group even thinking about competing for a top spot in the *mariachi* hierarchy.

Perhaps searching for a way to achieve the pinnacle of success dominated by the Vargas-Fuentes combo, some top groups immigrated to the United States in the 1950s and immediately had an influence on *mariachi* north-of-the-border. Los Angeles was probably their major target market because of its huge expatriate Mexican population. **Nati Cano** and his group, *Los Camperos*, achieved the most notable early success. There seemed to be a consensus among Hispanics and non-Hispanics alike that they were the best and most well-known U.S.-based *mariacheros* (a commonly used synonym for members of a *mariachi* group). Toward the end of the decade, *Los Camperos* opened *La Fonda*, a restaurant and nightclub in Los Angeles that became a permanent home for the group and the first American venue to exclusively showcase *mariachi*. U.C.L.A. also pioneered *mariachi* music education with the foundation of its Institute of Ethnomusicology and its very successful, cleverly named, group, *Mariachi Uclatlán*.

The 1960s were a decade of important milestones for *mariachi*. A Canadian priest, Father **Juan Marco LeClerc,** created the first Roman Catholic *Mariachi* Mass, called, aptly enough, *Misa Panamericana (The Pan American Mass)*. This folk mass, with Spanish lyrics and original music played by traditional *mariachi* instruments, covers all the elements of the service: *Angelus, Kyrie Eleison, Gloria, Alleluia, Offertory, Credo, Sanctus*, and *Agnus Dei.* The mass was completed in 1961, but was not celebrated until 1966. Its initial exposure in a small chapel in Cuernavaca was so successful that it had to be moved, on a regular basis, to that city's main cathedral. To this day it is not only celebrated throughout Mexico, but also in many areas of the United States where Mexican-Americans make up a large percentage of the population.

The second example of North American musical influences crossing borders came in 1962, when a Southern California musician, working out of a humble recording studio in his garage, experienced a severe case of "composer's block." He decided to take a break and head down to Tijuana to take in a bullfight. As he tells it, "... Something in the excitement of the crowd, the traditional *mariachi* music, the trumpet call heralding the start of the fight, the yelling, the snorting of the bulls, it all clicked. When we got back, I rearranged *'Twinkle Star,'* giving it a *mariachi* flavor and tempo...and added the authentic bullfight crowd noises." He renamed the tune *"The Lonely Bull,"* decided to call his group "The Tijuana Brass" and the "new sound" he had created *"ameriachi."* Six months later, **Herb Alpert's** initial offering had sold close to a million records and, during the next decade, his music did much to popularize what he called "the Tijuanal sound."

The sound was catchy and fresh, but it was definitely not *mariachi*. Harmonizing trumpets played the melody line, giving it a vaguely *mariachi* feel; but the rest of the instrumentation - piano, drums, and mandolins - was definitely a hybrid. Alpert was quick to point out that he had not perfected the *mariachi* sound; he had created a middle-of-the-road North American version of it. When he disbanded the group less than ten years later, he had released fifteen Tijuana Brass albums and had parlayed his original idea into a career as a media mogul. He retired as CEO of the hugely successful A & M

21

Records when European entertainment giant, Polygram, acquired it.

The 1970s were a decade that produced major watersheds in *mariachi* history. For instance, the year 1971 saw the formation of Arizona's first major Mexican-American *mariachi* group, *Mariachi Cobre*. *Mariachi* groups had even been formed in such far-flung parts of the globe as Japan and Europe. At the end of the decade, the First International *Mariachi* Conference was held in San Antonio, Texas. This gathering of experts attempted to identify and unite the disparate worldwide *mariachi* influences. The movement continues even today. The real breakthroughs, however, were made almost simultaneously by two gifted musicians—a young man living South of the Border and a young woman residing in the United States.

Juan Gabriel made his mark in Mexico, climbing from abject poverty and a childhood spent in an orphanage, to a pinnacle rarely achieved by any popular musician. This prolific songwriter/performer, with over 500 songs to his credit, reached the top with his composition *Amor Eterno*. He wrote this song, released in 1974, in memory of his late mother. It has since become an anthem for all mothers, his personal paean to the unrequited love he feels for his own. Gabriel still tours, records, composes, and performs while continuing to devote a great deal of his time to supporting an orphanage, located in Ciudad de México, that feeds, clothes, and provides a nurturing musical education for 140 children.

Women and Mariachi

Although it has been a widely held misconception in this country that women in *mariachi* were a "symbol of the '90s" and virtually non-existent in Mexico prior to then, the reality was considerably different. **Laura Sobrino** did much to crumble the gender barricade in the USA during the 1970s but she was not the only one. There is valid documentation of all-female groups playing in Mexico as far back as the 1940s. These pioneers included Mariachi Las Coroneles, Mariachi Las Adelitas, Mariachi Michoacana, and Mariachi Las Estrellas de México. Sobrino is a classically trained Mexican-American violinist who fell in love with *mariachi* while earning her music degree at the University of California, Santa Cruz. She was definitely influenced by **Rebecca Gonzales**, the first female member and a violinist, too, of Mariachi Los Camperos de Nati Cano. In 1975, Sobrino visited La Fonda (the famous club in Los Angeles where this group was based) to hear Gonzales perform. This was the beginning of a long and storied career.

Sobrino is not only a great musician, she is also an ethnomusicologist and a gifted transcriber; according to the *Los Angeles Times,* she is widely recognized as "The Queen of the *Mariachi.*" She was honored when she was selected as a Master Teacher by the prestigious foundation, the National Endowment of the Arts. In 1990, the city of Los Angeles unanimously acclaimed her as "Latina of the Year." Her all-female group, the highly praised Mujer 2000, regularly performs before thousands of fans at venues all across the United States. In June 2004, Sobrino and Gonzales were inducted into the International *Mariachi* Hall of Fame in Tucson, Arizona. It is leaders like both of these women, deeply immersed in the marrow of the music, who will teach both genders of the next generation of *mariachi* what they will need to succeed.

In 1987, *mariachi* as a global force took a quantum leap forward when yet another woman, **Linda Ronstadt**, released a tremendously popular recording called *Canciones de Mi Padre (Songs of My Father).* Shortly thereafter, Ronstadt embarked on a worldwide tour promoting her wonderful vocal renditions of the songs her father had taught her. The album was produced, arranged, and conducted by the protean Rubén Fuentes. Some of the musicians who were featured on this artistically and commercially successful effort included Mariachi Vargas, Mariachi Los Camperos de Nati Cano, Mariachi Los Galleros de Pedro Rey, and Mariachi Sol de México de Jose Hernandez. The tremendous interest in this initial effort had worldwide audiences clamoring for a sequel.

In 1991, the follow-up album, *Más Canciones (More Songs),* was released. The talents of Rubén Fuentes, Mariachi Vargas, and Los Camperos de Nati Cano once more were paired with Ronstadt's vocals. Music fans around the world were definitely taking notice of Mexico's wonderful folk music.

Thanks to the efforts of intrepid innovators like Rebecca Gonzales and Laura Sobrino, as well as those of courageous collaborators like Linda Ronstadt, *mariachi* is no longer exclusively the purview of men.

In 1994, Mexico finally recognized the importance of its country's contribution to world music when it hosted the International *Mariachi* Conference, fifteen years after the initial gathering in San Antonio. Since that time, while there have been a few unique groups attempting to revive a universal interest in the music—the efforts of Sol de México in California, first discovered on the album *Canciones de Mi Padre*, and the Texas-based group Campanas de America come to mind—the real vitality in the music will probably continue to spring from the grass roots efforts of the people of Mexico and the Mexican-American citizens of the United States.

Final Pop Quiz Review

Now that you have had a taste of the history of *mariachi*, let's review the answers in the quiz that opened this chapter to see how much your preconceived notions regarding *mariachi* have changed by increasing your knowledge.

The correct answers are A, B, C, F, G, H, I, K, and M. Regardless of your score, I suggest that you visit a neighborhood cantina that features great food, drink, and *mariachi*. Take along this little book and have some fun putting your newly found knowledge of *mariachi* to good use.

Bien hecho, amigos (well done, friends).

¡Hasta la vista!

Frequently Asked Questions and Mariachi Protocol
A Conversation with Laura Sobrino

Webster's New World Dictionary, Third College Edition, defines "protocol" as "the ceremonial forms accepted as correct in official dealings." What could protocol possibly have to do with a group of Americans listening to a *grupo* of Mexicans playing folk music? The best answer would probably be to place you, the reader, in a not-difficult-to-imagine, hypothetical situation. Let's have you and your *amigos* heading out for an evening of good food and frivolity at a local Mexican restaurant. Soon after the *nachos* and *salsa* and a pitcher of *margaritas* have arrived, your minds are on vacation and your mouths are working overtime. You find yourself tapping the table top in rhythm to the spicy sounds of the strolling *mariachi* that are now heading toward your group. You just love this music and you're really impressed. As the musicians get closer you begin to wonder, "What do we do now?"

Countless *gringos,* myself included, have asked themselves this very same question, as well as several others that naturally follow. You probably don't know all the answers yet! Let's see if we, the author and his authority, *mariachera* Laura Sobrino, can help.

Question: Do we stop eating and drinking when the *mariachi* arrive at our table? Should we continue the cessation of these activities throughout their performance? What if our *bebidas* (drinks) are getting warm and/or our *caldo* (soup) is getting cold?

Laura Sobrino: This always depends on the situation. What one should always do initially is to acknowledge the group's arrival to your area. You can do this with subtle eye contact, verbally, or by welcoming them with physical gestures. You are not "interrupting" the musical performance if you do any of these while the *mariachi* are playing and strolling towards your table. It is not necessary to stop eating or talking during the musicians' approach as long as you have acknowledged their presence. Of course, audience participation during the performance is definitely appreciated. If the group is playing a love song and you feel romantically inclined, feel free to hold hands or move closer to your companion. Besides making your evening more enjoyable, these outward manifestations of affection also let the *mariachi* know that you have appreciated their musical efforts.

Q: How do we know if the musicians are employed by the restaurant or are "free agents?" Does this impact on whether we should pay them, or whether the restaurant has hired them to entertain its patrons?

LS: If the group plays a song at your table and you have not made a prior payment arrangement, the musicians were probably hired by the restaurant to perform at different tables during their set. In any case, it would probably be wise to ask before they start playing. If the group is being compensated by the house to perform for its clientele's enjoyment, you are not obligated to tip but can supply a gratuity after the song is performed, requested or not.

Q: How do we know what to pay the musicians for their services? Do we pay by the song or by the amount of time they spend at our table? Is the fee based on the number of musicians in the group? Is it proper to ask any (or all) of these questions before they start playing, or do we play "Let's Make a Deal" when they're finished?

LS: The financial arrangements should be concluded *before* the music begins. If you decide to request a song for your table, it is not "uncouth" to inquire whether the group plays for tips of if they charge a flat fee per song. If their leader confirms the latter, you need to ask "how much per song?" If the fee is agreeable to both parties, you can then make your request and pay after the performance. If the group is compensated only by tips, then the proper gratuity depends on the number of musicians and how much you've enjoyed their music. A one dollar tip given to a solo musician or a group of musicians will be taken as an insult. A more appropriate tip would be $5 per song requested— or more, if you are especially pleased by the performance.

Q: What do I do if the musicians don't know the song I've requested? Can I hum a few bars? And if that attempt is still unsuccessful, do I then request another, or ask them to play something that they know?

LS: Sometimes the titles of the songs get confused by either the client or the musicians, so, yes, it does help to clearly identify your request if you can hum even a part of the melody. Most *mariachi* make it their responsibility to have perfected a large repertoire for the enjoyment of their customers, but if you find that you have "stumped the experts" on your first request, try making another. If they don't seem to know any of your requests (highly unlikely), ask them to play something that is one of their favorites. Consider suggesting a *style* of song such as "traditional" or "romantic," or even "up-beat" or "slow."

Q: Is it proper to request a song that they've played just a few minutes before, for another table, if I really want to hear it again?

LS: *Mariachi* definitely believe that the paying customers are always in control of what is to be played next. However, in my opinion, if guests are requesting *La Bamba* or a similar popular melody over and over again, they're missing one of the true strengths of the genre: a vast repertoire. Many groups pride themselves on knowing and professionally performing over 1500 songs! If your request is a birthday song, or another special occasion melody, of course you can request it all night. Locals sometimes will repeatedly request a song throughout the evening (at private parties, you see this even more frequently) since the *mariachi* philosophy is "you pay, we play."

Q: Is it proper for us to sing along with the performers and/or keep time by tapping, clapping, stomping, etc?

LS: The saying "When in Rome…" applies here, especially if you are in Mexico. Many times you will observe some customers singing along throughout the entire song. In fact, maybe everyone in the room will do this! It is not considered extraordinary when this happens. It is even acceptable for couples to dance along with the song, as long as they are not up on the tabletops, clenching roses in their teeth while attempting to shout *"Ole!"* Clapping along with the rhythms is often more difficult because of the complicated syncopations inherent in the music. The most traditional participation from the audience is the *"grito"* or yell, which is inserted at emotionally strategic moments during the performance. Different song forms have different *"gritos."* Use your judgment as to when to join in and let it come from deep inside your belly. Just keep in mind that you wouldn't want to yell "Yee-hah" in the middle of a poignant love ballad. Save your *grito* for boisterous numbers, nationalistic anthems and out-and-out drinking songs.

Q: How do I handle inattentive people in our party? And what can I do about inattentive people at another table, especially if their rude behavior is interfering with our enjoyment of the performance?

LS: I advise you to use common sense, which, all too often, is uncommon. Handle these situations in the same manner that you would usually handle them when they occur as part of a private, yet public, gathering.

Q: Is it admissible to request a solo by an individual member of the *mariachi* group if I particularly like that person's singing voice or abilities on his or her instrument? Will this cause bruised feelings within the group, especially if I wish to give the special performer an additional fee for this extra effort?

LS: Not a problem. The group thinks and functions as a group, not as a loose collection of individual performers. If a special request is made to a particular group member, the entire group takes pride that you are enjoying their collective performance. They also appreciate any special generosity you might bestow upon them.

Q: Can I request songs that are not traditionally part of the *mariachi* repertoire? A trio of sample "borderline" tunes comes to mind: *Vaya con Dios* by Les Paul and Mary Ford, *Lemon Tree* by Trini Lopez, and *Spanish Flea* by the Tijuana Brass. Does "pushing the envelope" hurt their feelings?

LS: Actually *Vaya con Dios* has become a standard in the *mariachi* repertoire. The musicians take great pride in an ever-expanding play list. If they receive many requests for songs by Trini Lopez or the TJ Brass, then they will make the effort to learn them. However, from my experience, it does not appear as though songs by these performers are heavily requested.

Q: If a member of my party wishes to perform a vocal solo with the group, is it permissible to ask the group to accompany him or her? Furthermore, is it permissible to request that the song be played in a key that will maximize the vocal strengths of the soloist? If this is a spur-of-the-moment occurrence, not pre-negotiated, how do we arrive at fair compensation for this special service?

LS: It is a standard practice, well within the *mariachi* tradition, for groups to accompany any singing client who wishes to stand up and perform. If the customer sticks to songs on the musicians' normal play list, the resulting performance will probably be very pleasing to all involved. Leave the key placement to the players. They have experience with the songs to know which key is appropriate for the singer. They may ask the singer to hum a particular line in the song that will identify his proper key within his range. If the key is inappropriate for the guest vocalist once the music has begun, it is not unusual for the group to make a "key adjustment" right in the middle of the song. Or, if the singer begins to drift "off-key," the *mariachi* are trained to adjust the key to match the new tonal home, wherever it is located. Finally, regarding the *dinero,* let your conscience be your guide, keeping in mind the almost universally acceptable unwritten rule of $5 per requested song.

Q: If the musicians are not pleasing to us, what is the least painful (and most expeditious way) to get them to move along?

LS: This situation should be handled with finesse, and is relatively easy if you just put yourself into the musicians' shoes for a moment. You need to acknowledge the group's arrival but then politely give them a "no thank you" look or softly say the words. Whether they are hired by the restaurant or are "free agents," it is their responsibility not to intrude on your enjoyment of the evening. They should respect your wishes. If all of these measures fail, you may use Mexico's almost universally recognized form of rejection: a raised forefinger accompanied by synchronized "east-to-west and back again" head wagging. This will transmit your message in the most unequivocal manner.

Q: If the *mariachi* are heading away from another table, is it permissible to send a member of our group to follow them and request a detour our way?

LS: If they are not approaching a break, the *mariachi* welcome anyone who wishes them to play at their table. The musicians want to know that they are being appreciated and that you enjoy their performance. If they are taken out of their normal route, it would definitely be appropriate to make it worth their while by offering them a special gratuity. This could even be given to them at the time that your party's member follows them to request a detour. Once again, $5 is the almost always acceptable amount.

Q: If the tempo at which our request is being played should be (in our humble opinion as the paying audience) faster or slower, is there a diplomatically acceptable means of making our wishes known?

LS: No! I have never seen or heard of a client "meddling" in the group's performance in this manner. I have had customers complain that a verse was inadvertently omitted or sung wrong, but never a request for a song to be played slower or faster. If you are displeased in any way, not requesting additional songs is the proper way to handle the situation.

Q: Let's say our party leaves *Cantina A* and heads to *Cantina B?* Lo and behold, the *mariachi* from *Cantina A* now appear in *Cantina B?* We loved them in *A* and showed our appreciation. But we are now immersed in a serious, personal conversation. How do we get this point across without hurting anybody's feelings?

LS: Just say "no thank you" when the group approaches your table. If *Cantina B*'s clientele is hiring the group song-by-song and the performance seems to go on-and-on, I would say that your chances of carrying on a personal conversation range from slim to none. You would probably be wise to leave if you want a quieter spot.

Q: A member of our party plays a "mean" guitar (and is a legend in his own mind). Is it appropriate for him to ask the *mariachi* who plays his instrument of choice to either "sit in" or borrow it to serenade the rest of us?

LS: No. Even though this is a "folk music," that doesn't necessarily mean that it is "easy." If your friend has had some training or exposure to Mexican music, you may want to talk to the group members and ask them if it is acceptable. You would probably be wise not to insist if they say "no." In my twenty plus years of experience as a professional *mariachera,* I have never seen my colleagues lend their instruments to anyone. However, each musician is the owner of his or her own instrument, and some may feel differently about this very personal matter.

Q: One of my *amigos* is having such a good time and is so taken with the *mariachi* that he or she offers to buy them a round of *cervezas.* Is this acceptable behavior?

LS: Yes, but I would ask the management first if this is allowed and then ask the group if they would accept the "gift." Some establishments don't allow the musicians to drink while others encourage it because of the additional sale of beverages. Some group directors have agreements with their *mariachi* not to over-drink, so your offer could be accepted or rejected based on what the musicians have already consumed by the time they reach your table.

Q: A night after hearing a wonderful group perform throughout dinner, we visit another eatery in the same town and are subjected to a less-than-professional band of ear-splitters. Is it acceptable to talk to the restaurant's proprietor about the excellence of the first group (we happen to have one of their business cards) and attempt to have the second group relocated to the great outdoors? What if the *maestro* of the second group is the restaurant owner's favorite uncle?

LS: The answer is, plain and simple, don't get involved. It is difficult for me as a professional musician to understand why you might think it is your right to go to a proprietor and talk about another group. I would never think of that. My simple advice is to enjoy your evening out, but not at someone else's expense.

In conclusion, the proper protocol for listening to *mariachi* is only of prime importance in a restaurant or *cantina* setting, where the musicians perform as a strolling orchestra inviting requests. Another very pleasant experience (without so many opportunities to interrelate) is attending a *mariachi* festival or concert where each of several groups plays a set of their very best efforts. There is an annual summer sit-down event at the Hollywood Bowl in Southern California that is usually sold out far in advance.

In Mexico, Guadalajara's Plaza Tlaquepaque and Ciudad de México's Plaza Garibaldi feature a "battle of the bands" format every weekend. Pick up some of your favorite *botanas* (snacks) and *bebidas* (beverages), spread a *serape* (blanket) on the grass, and join the revelers. You won't be sorry you did. If you are not certain if the Mexican town you're visiting has a weekly *mariachi* venue, the *concierge* at your hotel can probably steer you in the right direction. Make sure this little volume you're presently reading accompanies you when you depart. It will very definitely make you feel comfortable anywhere *mariachi* are playing.

You are now armed with the correct procedures for almost any eventuality that could occur. These will definitely identify you as an expert in the field.

¡Gozar! (Enjoy!)

The Top 50 Mariachi Selections
How They Were Chosen

When I initially began my quest for *Mariachi's* Top 50, I confused many of the ethnomusicologists I contacted when I told them I was searching for *mariachi* "anthems." My respondents wrote back asking what I meant. This forced me to define what I was looking for in much clearer terms. I replied that I was looking for the most popular, most requested songs. The return queries asked, in effect, "Most popular and most requested by whom?"

It finally dawned on me that what I was really looking for were the most popular, most requested *mariachi* standards from the point of view of the Hispanic community. As a *gringo* myself, I wanted to know what the Mexican people considered their most beloved songs. After all, since they had created the music, they could unequivocally "show me the way," correct?

Not exactly! What I hadn't accounted for were regional differences. Just as Americans in Texas might prefer country and western tunes more than New Englanders, Mexicans in coastal Veracruz were more partial to their local music (*sones veracruzanos*) than they were to the music of, say, Sonora, the home of Mexico's finest cattle, where *rancheras* led the "Hit Parade." To find the "real" Top 50, I decided to poll a cross section of *mariachi*, educators, ethnomusicologists, and fans of both genders, living both north and south of the border. The songs that appeared on the most ballots were then numerically weighted (the sum of a song's individual ranking score divided by the number of respondents) to arrive at the list finally used. This list appears at the end of this section. Following the list, the songs are arranged alphabetically with their numeric ranking as well as the tempo or type of song (*bolero, huapango, ranchera,* etc.). On the left is the lead sheet for each song, featuring an annotated melody line, chord symbols, and Spanish lyrics. On the right, you will find the Spanish lyrics as well as a line-by-line English translation of the story. Idiomatic expressions in English may also be included.

If you're going out for a night on the town featuring *mariachi* you should not leave home without this book. But the book will also give you much pleasure if you decide to play the music on a piano or guitar wherever and whenever you can. People who have told me that they didn't particularly care for *mariachi* have been amazed when they've heard me play, for instance, *Sabor a Mi.* When I told them what they were listening to (a *bolero*, a true *mariachi* standard), another preconception began to disappear as they admitted they genuinely enjoyed the tune. (This was equally amazing to me because I am not that good of a pianist!)

What's next? Perhaps *mariachi karaoke* is not an impossibility.

The next time you're at a cantina and a *mariachero* asks you what you'd like to hear, you'll have 50 choices—not just *La Bamba*!

The
Top 50
Mariachi Songs

Amor

Tempo di Beguine C

Gabriel Ruiz & Ricardo Lopez Mendez

A - mor, a- mor, a - mor,____ Na - ció de ti, Na - ció de mi, de la es - pe - ran - za.____ A -

mor, a - mor, a - mor,____ na - ció de Dios pa - ra los dos, Na - cio del al - ma.____ Sen -

tir que tus be - sos a ni - da- ron en mí, I-gual que pa - lo-mas men-sa-je-ras de luz. Sa -

ber que mis be- sos se que- da- ron en ti, hacien-do_en tus la-bios la se ñal de las cruz. A -

mor, a- mor, a - mor,____ na - ció de ti, na - ció de mi, de la es - pe -

ran - za.____ A-mor, a - mor, a - mor, Na - ció de

Dios, pa - ra los dos, Na - ció del al - ma.____ A -

al - ma,____ a - mor,____ a - mor,____

Amor

Spanish Lyrics	English Translation
Amor, Amor, Amor, nació de ti, nació de mí,	Love, Love, Love, born of you, born of me,
De la esperanza.	Of the hope.
Amor, Amor, Amor, nació de Dios, para los dos,	Love, Love, Love, born of God, for us both,
Nació del alma.	Born of the soul.
Sentir que tus besos a nidaron en mí,	To feel that your kisses have a nest in me,
Igual que palomas mensajeras de luz,	Like doves, messengers of light,
Saber que mis besos se quedaron en ti haciendo	To know that my kisses stayed in you making
En tus labios la señal de la cruz.	In your lips the sign of the cross.
Amor, Amor, Amor, nació de ti, nació de mí	Love, Love, Love, born of you, born of me,
De la esperanza.	Of the hope.
Amor, Amor, Amor, nació de Dios, para los dos,	Love, Love, Love, born of God, for us both,
Nació del alma.	Born of the soul.
Amor, Amor.	Love, Love.

Aquellos Ojos Verdes

42

Aquellos Ojos Verdes   *Utrera-Menendez*

Spanish Lyrics	English Translation
Fueron tus ojos los que me dierón	It was your eyes that gave me
El tema dulce de mi canción.	The sweet theme of my song.
Tus ojos verdes claros serenos,	Your clear green serene eyes,
Ojos que hansido mi inspiración.	Eyes that have been my inspiration.
Aquellos ojos verdes	Those green eyes
De mira da serena	Of serene sight
Dejaron en mi alma	Left my soul
Eterna sed de amar.	(An) eternal thirst for love (divine).
Anhelos de caricias	(The) desire of (your) caress
De besos y ternuras	Of kisses and tenderness
De todas las dulzuras	Of all the sweetness
Que sabían brindar.	That (you) knew how to offer,
Aquellos ojos verdes,	Those green eyes,
Serenos como un lago	Serene as a (deep) lake,
En cuyas quietas aguas	In whose calm waters
Un día me miré	One day I saw myself (my reflection).
No saben las tristezas	They don't know the sadness
Que en mi alma han dejado	That (they left) in my soul.
Aquellos ojos verdes,	Those green eyes
Que yo nunca besaré	That I will never kiss.

¡Ay, Jalisco No Te Rajes!

Corrido Lento — Cortazar-Esperon

Lyrics (as underlaid in the music):

¡Ay! Ja-lis-co, Ja-lis-co, Ja-lis-co tú tie-nes tu no-via que es Gua-da-la-ja-ra.

Mu-cha-cha bo-ni-ta, la per-la más ra-ra de to-do Ja-lis-co es mi Gua-da-la-ja-ra.

1. ¡Ay

2. Y me Ja-lis-co no te ra-jes! me sa-le del al-ma gri-tar con ca-lor, a-brir to-do el pe-cho pá e-char es-te gri-to: ¡Qué lin-do es Ja-lis-co, pa-la-bra de ho-nor!

44

¡Ay, *Jalisco No Te Rajes!* *Cortazar-Esperon*

Spanish Lyrics	English Translation
¡Ay!, Jalisco, Jalisco, Jalisco,	Oh! Jalisco, Jalisco, Jalisco
Tú tienes tu novía que es Guadalajara.	You have your girlfriend which is *Guadalajara.*
Muchacha bonita, la perla más rara	Pretty girl, the most rare pearl
De todo Jalisco,es mi Guadalajara.	In all of *Jalisco,* is my *Guadalajara.*
Y me gusta escuchar los mariachis,	And I like to hear the *mariachis,*
Cantar con el alma tus lindas canciones;	And sing with my soul your beautiful songs;
Oir como suenan esos guitarrónes	And listen to how those bass guitars sound
Y echarme un tequila con los valentones.	And have myself a *tequila* with the brave ones.
¡Ay! Jalisco no te rajes!	Oh! *Jalisco*, don't quit!
Me sale del alma gritar con calor,	It comes from my soul to shout with passion
Abrir todo el pecho pa' echar este grito:	Open wide my breast to utter this shout:
¡Qué lindo es Jalisco,palabra de honor!	How beautiful *Jalisco* is, this is my oath!
Pa' mujeres Jalisco primero,	The women of *Jalisco* are first
Lo mismo en los Altos que allá	The same (first) in the hills as
en la Cañada;	in the ravines;
Mujeres muy lindas, rechulas de cara,	Very beautiful women with pretty faces,
Asi son las hembras de Guadalajara.	That's how the women are in *Guadalajara.*
En Jalisco se quiere a la Buena,	In *Jalisco* you love for the good
Porque es peligrosa quere allá mala,	Because it is dangerous to love in a bad way,
Por una morena echar mucha balas	For a brunette, fire off many bullets
Y baja la luna cantar en Chapala	And sing in *Chapala*, under the moon.
¡Ay! Jalisco, Jalisco, Jalisco,	Oh, *Jalisco, Jalisco, Jalisco*
Tus hombres con machos	Your men are "real men"
y son cumplidores	And are reliable,
Valientes y ariscos y sostenedores	Brave, and rough and supporting.
No admiten rivales en cosas de amores	Don't accept rivals in matters of love.
Es tu orgullo tu traje de charro,	Your *charro* (cowboy) suit is your pride,
Traer tu pistola fajada en el cinto,	To have your gun tucked in your belt,
Tener tu guitarra pá echar mucho tipo	And to have your guitar to impress the girls
Y a los que presumen quitarles	And for those who boast of "taking away"
el hipo.	the hiccups.

Bésame Mucho

Bésame Mucho   *Velasquez*

Spanish Lyrics	English Translation
Bésame, bésame mucho,	Kiss me, kiss me a lot,
Como si fuera esta noche la última vez.	As though this night was the last time.
Bésame, bésame mucho,	Kiss me, kiss me a lot,
Que tengo miedo, perderte, perderte otra vez.	Because I'm so scared of losing you, of losing you in other ways.
Quiero tenerte muy cerca,	I want to have you very close,
Mirar me en tus ojos,	To see myself in your eyes,
verte junto a mí.	see you close to me.
Piensa, que tal vez mañana	Just think that maybe tomorrow
Yo, ya estaré lejos,	I, I'll be far,
Muy lejos de ti...	Very far from you...
Bésame , bésame mucho	Kiss me, kiss me a lot,
Como si fuera este noche la última vez,	As though this night was the last time.
Bésame, bésame mucho,	Kiss me, kiss me a lot,
Que tengo miedo, perderte, perderte después.	Because I'm so afraid of losing you, of losing you afterward.

Camino Real de Colima

A Son From the State of Colima

1.Ca - mi - no Re -al - de Co li - ma,   no me qui -si e ra a - cor - dar
2.To - mo la plu - ma en la ma no,   pa - ra es - cri - bir y fir - mar

Ca - mi - no Re - al - de Coli - ma,   no me qui -si e ra a - cor - dar
To - mo la plu - ma en la ma no,   pa - ra es - cri - bir y fir - mar

Los   tra - ba - jos que_ pa - se_ en e - se ca - mi - no re - al.

Los   tra - ba - jos que_ pa - se_ en e - se

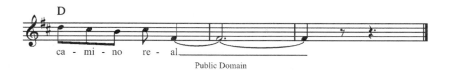

ca - mi - no re - al.

48

Ranking: #39   # Camino Real de Colima   *Anon*

Spanish Lyrics	English Translation
Camino Real de Colima *No me quisiera acordar* *(2 x's)*	The Royal Road of *Colima* I should not like to recall (2 x's)
Los trabajos que pas *En ese camino real* *(2 x's)*	The workers that pass On that royal road (2 x's)
Tomo la pluma en al mano *Para escribir y firmar* *(2 x's)*	I take the pen in my hand To write and to sign (my name) (2 x's)
Los trabajos que pasé *En ese Camino Real* *(2 x's)*	The workers that pass On that royal road (2 x's)

Chiapanecas

50

Chiapanecas

DeCampo

Spanish Lyrics	English Translation
Un clavel corté	I cut a carnation.
Por la sierra fui	Over the mountains down
caminito de mi rancho	the little road on my ranch
Como el viento fue en caballo fiel	Like the wind was my faithful horse
A llevarme hasta tu lado	To take me to your side.
Linda flor de abril toma este clavel	Lovely April flower, take this carnation
Que te brindo compasión	That I offer you with compassion.
No me digas no que	Don't tell me, "No," because that,
en tu boca está	in your mouth, is
El secreto de mi amor!	The secret of my love!
Cuando la noche llegó	When the night came
Y con su manto de azul	And with her cloak (mantle) of blue
El blanco rancho cubrió	Covered the white ranch,
Alegre el baile empezó	Happily, the dance began.
Baila mi Chiapaneca	Dance, my (little) girl from *Chiapas.*
Baila, baila con garbo	Dance, dance with grace,
Baila suave rayo de luz	Dance, gentle ray of light
Baila mi Chiapaneca	Dance, my (little) girl from *Chiapas,*
Baila, baila con garbo	Dance, dance with grace,
Que en el baile	That at the dance
Reina eres tú Chiapaneca gentil.	You are Queen, my gentle *Chiapaneca.*

Cielito Lindo

Mexican Folk Song

Public Domain

Cielito Lindo

Anon

Spanish Lyrics	English Translation
De la Sierra Morena,	The dark mountains give,
Cielito Lindo,	Beautiful sky,
Vienen bajando.	Many things of interest.
Un par de ojitos negros,	One from the black eyes,
Cielito Lindo,	Beautiful sky,
De contrabando.	Of the smuggler.
¡Ay, ay, ay, ay!	Oh, oh, oh, oh!
Canta y no llores;	Sing and don't cry;
Porque cantando se a alegran,	Because singers are happy,
Cielito Lindo,	Beautiful sky,
Los corazónes.	In their hearts.
Pájaro que abandona	The bird that flew away from
Su primer nido,	Its first nest,
Su primer nido	Its first nest,
Si lo encuentra ocupado,	Yes, it finds a place to live,
Cielito Lindo,	Beautiful sky,
Bien merecido.	That's good and worthy.
!Ay, ay, ay, ay!	Oh, oh, oh, oh!
Mira primero,	Look first,
Y donde pones los ojos,	And where your eyes look,
Cielito Lindo,	Beautiful sky,
No llores luego.	There'll soon be no tears.

Cocula

Corrido

Cortazar-Esperon

De es-ta tie-rra de Co-cu-la que es el al-ma del ma-ria-chi ven-go yo con mi can-tar, Voy ca-mi-no a Aguas-ca-lien-tes a la Fe-ria de San Mar-cos, a ver lo qué pue-do ha-llar Trai-go un - De Co-cu-la es el ma-ria-chi de Te-ca-ti-tlán los so-nes, de San Pe-dro su can-tar de Te-qui-la su mez-cal y los ma-chos de Ja-lis-co a-fa-ma-dos por en tro-nes, por e-so tra en pan-ta-lo-nes.

Cocula

Spanish Lyrics	English Translation
De esta tierra de Cocula	Of this land of *Cocula*,
Que es el alma del mariachi,	That is the soul of the mariachi,
Vengo yo con mi cantar,	I come with my song,
Voy camino a Aguascalientes	I'm on the road to *Aguascalientes*,
A la Feria de San Marcos	To the Fair of *San Marcos*,
A ver lo qué puedo hallar.	To see what I can find.
Traigo un gallo muy jugado	I bring a very experienced rooster
Para echarlo de tapado	To compete
Con algun apostador,	With those backed by some other bettors,
Y también traigo pistola	And I also bring a pistol
Por si alguno busca bola	In case somebody looks for a fight
Y me tilda de hablador.	And labels me a talker.
De Cocula es el mariachi	In *Cocula* there is the *mariachi*
De Tecatitlán los sones	In *Tecatitlán* there are the songs
De San Pedro su cantar,	In *San Pedro* there is singing,
De Tequila su mezcal	In *Tequila* there is *mezcal*
Y los machos Jalisco	And the *"machos"* of *Jalisco*
Afamados por entrones,	Famous for being ruffians
Por eso tra en pantalones.	That's why they wear the pants.
Vengo en busca de una ingrata	I come in search of an ingrate,
De una joven presumida	Of a young, conceited, girl
Que se fue con mi querer,	Who left with my love;
Traigo ganas de encontraria	I feel like finding her
Pa' enseñarle que de un hombre	To show her that I am a man who
No se burla una mujer.	A woman does not make fun of.
Se me vino de repente	It came to me suddenly,
Dando pie pa' que la gente	Repenting so that the people
Murmurara porque sí,	Would murmur like they do,
Pero a ver hoy que la encuentra	But let's see today if I can find her,
Y quedemos frente a frente	And we stand face-to-face.
Qué me va adecir a mí.	What's she going to say to me?
De Cocula es el mariachi.	In *Cocula* there is the *mariachi*.

Cuando Calienta El Sol

Carlos Rigual, Mario Rigual & Carlos Martinoli

Mod. Slow/Bolero

Cuan-do ca-lien-ta el sol_ a-quí en la pla-ya,_

Sien-to tu cuer-po vi-brar cer-ca de mí,_

es tu pal-pi-tar_ es tu ca-ra_ es tu pe-lo_ son tus

be-sos,_ me es-tre-mez-co_ o-o-o;

Cuan-do ca-lien-ta el sol_ a-quí en la pla-ya,_

sien-to tu cuer-po vi-brar cer-ca de mí,_

es tu pal-pi-tar_ tu re-cuer-do_ mi lo-cu-ra_ mi de-

li-rio_ me es-tre-mez-co_ o-o-o, Cuan-do ca-lien-ta el

1. sol._

2. sol._

56

Cuando Calienta El Sol *Rigual-Martinoli*

Spanish Lyrics	English Translation

Cuando calienta el sol aquí en la playa,
Siento tu cuerpo vibrar cerca de mi;
Es tu palpitar, es tu cara, es tu pelo,
Son tus besos, me estremezco, o, o, o!

When the sun heats up here on the beach,
I feel your body quiver next to mine;
Trembling - it's your face, it's your hair,
It's your kisses, I tremble, oh, oh, oh!

Cuando calienta el sol aquí en la playa,
Siento tu cuerpo vibrar cerca de mí,
Es tu palpitar, tu recuerdo, mi locura,
Mi delirio, me estremezco, o, o, o!

When the sun heats up here on the beach,
I feel your body quiver next to me,
Trembling - your remembrance, my madness,
My delirium, I tremble, oh, oh, oh!

Cuando calienta el sol aquí en la playa,
Cerca de mi es tu palpitar.

When the sun heats up here on the beach,
Next to me, trembling.

(Se repite)

(Repeats)

Cuando Vuelva a Tu Lado

58

Cuando Vuelva a Tu Lado *Grever*

Spanish Lyrics	English Translation
¿Recuerdas aquel beso	Do you remember that kiss
Que en broma me negarste?	That you (so)crudely refused me?
Se escapó de tus labios	It escaped from your lips
Sin querer.	Without desire.
Asustado por ello	I was afraid to seek
Buscó abrigo.	Shelter in that (kiss).
En la inmensa amargura,	I'm immensely bitter,
De mi ser.	I am.
Cuando vuelva a tu lado,	When I return to your side,
No me niegues tus besos.	Don't deny me your kisses.
Que el amor	(I know) that the love
que te he dado,	that I have given you,
No podrás olvidar.	You will never forget.
No me preguntes nada,	Don't ask me anything,
Que nada he	(Because) I am not going
de explicarte.	to explain anything to you.
Que el beso que negarste,	(That) the kiss that you denied me,
Ya no lo puedes dár.	You can't give (to) me any more.
Cuando vuelva a tu lado,	When I return to your side,
Y esté sola contigo,	And (I) am alone with you,
Las cosas que te digo,	The things that I tell you,
No repitas jamás,	Don't repeat ever,
por compasíon.	for compassion (for me).
Une tu labio al mio,	Join your lips to mine,
Y estrachame en tus bravos,	And embrace me in your arms,
Y cuenta los latidos	And count the beats
De nuestra corazón.	Of our hearts.

Cucurrucucú Paloma

Di - cen que por las no - ches no - más se le i - ba en pu - ro llo - rar,

di - cen que no co - mí - a no - más se le i - ba en pu - ro to - mar,

ju - ran que el mis -mo cie - lo se es -tre -me cí - a al o - ir su llan - to;____

co -mo su -frió por e -lla que has-ta en su muer -te la fué lla -man -do_____ ay, ay, ay, ay,

ay,_____ can - ta - ba,____ ay, ay, ay, ay,

ay,_____ ge - mí - a,____ ay, ay, ay, ay,

mo - res, Cu - cu - rru - cu - cú,____ cu - cu - rru - cu - cú,

ten ten ten

cu -cu -rru -cu - cú____ pa - lo -ma ya no le llo - res.__

Cucurrucucú Paloma   *Mendez*

Spanish Lyrics	English Translation
Dicen qué por las noches	This is what is for the evenings,
Nomás se le iba en puro llorar,	Just to know that it was a pure cry,
Dicen qué no comía,	This is not for eating,
Nomás se le iba en puro tomar;	Just to know that it was a pure drink;
Juran que el mismo cielo	To swear that the same sky
Se estreme cia al oir su llanto;	Shakes to hear your weeping;
Como sufrió por ella	How I suffered for her,
Que hasta en su muerte la fué llamando.	How her death has kept me away & busy.
¡Ay ay ,ay ,ay, ay...cantaba!	Oh oh, oh, oh, oh...your singing!
¡Ay ay, ay,ay, ay...gemía!	Oh oh, oh, oh ,oh...your moaning!
¡Ay ay, ay, ay, ay...cantaba	Oh oh, oh, oh, oh...your singing!
¡De passion mortal...moria!	The fatal emotion...your dying!
Qué una paloma triste,	What a sad dove,
Muy de manaña la va a cantar,	Singing so much to you in the morning,
A la casita sola	Alone in her little house
Con las puertitas de par en par;	With her little doors wide open;
Juran que esa paloma	A dove pledges that
No es otra cosa	There is nothing (worth)
más que su alma,	more than a soul,
Que todaviá la espera	That (there) is still the hope
A que regrese	That she will come back from
la desdichada.	her unlucky fate.
¡Cucurrucucú,...paloma!	Cooing...the dove!
¡Cucurrucucú,...no llores!	Cooing...don't cry!
¡Las piedras jamás,...paloma,	The everlasting stone, the dove
¡Que van a saber de amores!	That knows the difference between loves!
¡Cucurrucucú!...¡cucurrucucú!	Cooing...cooing!
¡Cucurrucucú...paloma!	Cooing...dove!
¡Ya no le llores!	Don't cry!

61

De Colores

Spanish Song

Moderato

1. De_____ co - lo - res,_____ de co - lo - res se vis - ten los
2. Can_____ ta el ga - llo,_____ can-ta el ga - llo con su qui - ri,

cam-pos en la pri - ma - ve - ra,_____ De_____ co - lo - res,_____ de co -
qui - ri, qui - ri, qui - ri, qui - ri,_____ La_____ ga - lli - na_____ la ga -

lo - res son los pa - ja - ri - tos que vie - nen de a - fue - ra._____
lli - na con su ca - ra, car - ra, car - ra, ca - ra, ca - ra._____

De_____ co - lo - res, de co - lo - res es el ar - co
Los_____ po - llue - los,_____ los po - llue - los con su pí - o,

i - ris que ve - mos lu - cir,_____ Y por
pí - o, pí - o, pí - o, pi,_____ Y por e - so los gran-des a -

mor-es de mu-chos co - lo-res me gus-tan a mí._____ Y por mí._____

De Colores

Spanish Lyrics	English Translation
De colores,	The colors,
De colores se visten	The colors I see,
los campos en la primavera,	the fields are clothed with in the spring,
De colores,	The colors,
De colores son los pajaritos	The colors, the little birds
que vienen de afuera.	that are from outside.
De colores,	The colors,
De colores es el arco iris que vemos lucir.	The colors of the rainbow that we see shine.
Y por eso los grandes amores	And that's why I have great love
De muchos colores me gustan a mí.	For the many colors that I like.
Y por eso los grandes amores	And that's why I have great love
De muchos colores me gustan a mí.	For the many colors that I like.
Canta el gallo	The rooster sings
Canta el gallo con su quiri, quiri, quiri,	The rooster sings with its "quiri, quiri, quiri."
La gallina,	The hen,
La gallina con su cara, cara, cara,	The hen with its "cara, cara, cara,"
Los polluelos,	The little chicks,
Los polluelos con su pío, pío, pío, pí.	The little chicks with their "pío, pío, pío, pí"
Y por eso los grandes amores...	And that's why I have great love...
De colores,	The colors,
De colores brillantes y finos aurora.	Of bright and fine colors that dress the dawn.
De colores,	The colors,
De colores son los mil reflejos	The colors that are a thousand reflections
Que el sól atesora.	That the sun treasures.
De colores,	The colors,
De colores se viste el diamante que	The colors I see, the diamond that
debo lucir.	I am to wear, sparkles.
Y por eso los grandes amores...	And that's why I have great love...

Dos Arbolitos

Ranchero

Chucho Martinez Gil

Han na-ci-do en mi ran-cho dos ar-bo-li - tos,_

dos ar-bo-li - tos que pa-re-cen ge-me-los;_

y des-de mi ca-si - ta los veo so-li - tos; ba jo el am-pa-ro san to y la luz del

cie - lo._ Nun-ca es-tán se-pa-ra-dos u-no del o - tro,_

por que a-sí qui-so Dios que los dos na - cie- ran,_ y con sus mis-mas

ra-mas se ha-cen ca - ri - cias co-mo si fue-ran no-vios que se qui-sie- ran._

Ar-bo-li-to ar-bo-li-to, ba-jo tu som-bra voy a es-pe rar que el dí-a can-sa-do mue - ra,

y cuan-do es-toy so-li-to mi-ran-do al cie lo, pi-do pa que me man-de u-na com-pa-

ñe-ra. Ar-bo-li-to, ar-bo-li-to, me sien-to so lo quie-ro que me a-com-

pa - ñes has-ta que mue - ra

Dos Arbolitos

Spanish Lyrics	English Translation

Han nacido en mi rancho
  dos arbolitos,
Dos arbolitos que paracen gemelos;
Y desde mi casita los
  veo solitos
Bajo el amparo santo
  y la luz del cielo.
	On my ranch two little trees
	  have been born,
	Two little trees that look like twins;
	And from my little house
	  I see them all alone
	Under the holy protection
	  and the light from heaven.

Nunca están separados
  uno del otro,
Porque así quiso
Dios que los dos nacieran,
	They are never separated
	  one from the other,
	Because that is how the
	Lord wanted them to be born,

Y con sus mismas ramas
  se hacen caricias
Como si fueran novios
  que se quisieran.
Arbolito, arbolito, bajo tu sombra
Voy a esperar que
  el día cansado muera,
	And with the same branches
	  they caress each other
	As if they were sweethearts
	  that loved each other.
	Little tree, little tree, under your shade
	I'm going to wait until
	  the end of this tiring day,

Y cuando estoy solito mirando al cielo,
Pido pa que me mande
  una compañera
Arbolito, arbolito, me siento solo
Quiero que me acompañes hasta que muera.
	And when I'm all alone looking at the sky,
	I'm going to ask heaven to send me
	  a companion.
	Little tree, little tree, I feel alone
	I want you to accompany me until I die.

El Mariachi

Corrido - Huapango

Pepe Guizar

El ma - ria - chi de mi tie - rra___ de mi tie - rra ta - pa - tí - a voy a dar le mi can - tar.___ A - rru - lla - do por sus so - nes___ se me c - ió la cu - ña mi - a se hi zo mi al - ma mu - si - cal.___ Sus vio - li - nes y gui - ta - rras___ en las quie - tas ma - dru - ga - das son un dul - ce quie - tas ma - dru - tar.___ Al - ma vir - gen___ del ma - ria - chi,___ del ma - cu - cho tus can - tar - es si - en to ga - nas de llo - rar. rar. El ma - ria - chi sue - ña___ con a - le - gre son,___ o - ye co - mo a - le - gra; can - ta mi can - ción.___ El ma - ria - chi ción. Sue - ña el ar - pa vie - ja___ sue - ña el gui - ta - rrón, el vio - lín se que - ja___ lo mis - mo que yo. Sue - ña el ar - pa lo mis - mo que yo.___ al 𝄋 y G7 Al ma - lo mis - mo que yo.___

El Mariachi

Guizar

Spanish Lyrics	English Translation

El mariachi de mi tierra,
De mi tierra tapatía.
Voy a darle mi cantar,
Arrulado por sus sones.
Se meció la cuña mia,
Se hizo mi alma musical.

The *mariachi* of my homeland,
Of my typical homeland.
I'm going to give him my song,
Caressed by its sounds.
My cradle rocked,
My soul became musical.

Sus violines y guitarras,
En las quietas madrugadas,
Son un dulce despertar.
Alma virgen del mariachi,
Cuando escucho tus cantares,
Siento ganas de llorar.

Your violins and guitars,
In the quiet dawn,
Are a sweet awakening.
Virgin soul of the *mariachi,*
When I hear your songs,
I feel like crying.

El mariachi sueña con alegre son.
Oye,como alegra
Canta mi canción.
Sueña el arpa vieja (¡ay! ¡ay! ¡ay)
Sueña el guitarrón (¡ay! ¡ay! ¡ay!)
El violín se queja (¡ay! ¡ay! ¡ay!
Lo mismo que yo.

The *mariachi* plays a happy tune.
Listen how it cheers you up
To sing my song.
The old harp plays (ay! ay! ay!)
The bass guitar plays (ay! ay! ay!)
The violin complains (ay! ay! ay!)
The same as I do.

El mariachi sueña con alegre son.

The *mariachi* plays a happy tune.

El Rancho Grande

Ranchero

Silvano R. Ramos

A - llá en el ran - cho gran - de, A - llá don - de vi - ví - a,

Ha - bía u - na ran - che - ri - ta, Que a - le - gre me de -

cí - a, Que a - le - gre me de - cí - a: Te voy a ha -

cer tus cal - zó - nes Co - mo los

u - sa el ran - che - ro; Te los co -

mien - zo de la - na, Te los a -

ca - bo de cue - ro.

El Rancho Grande   *Ramos*

Spanish Lyrics	English Translation

Allá en al rancho grande,
Allá donde vivía,
Había una rancherita
Que alegre me decía,
Que alegre me decía,

(Out) there on the big ranch,
(Out) there where I once lived,
There was a little ranch girl
Who would happily tell me,
Who would happily tell me,

Te voy hacer tus calzónes
Como los usa el ranchero.
Te los comienzo de lana,
Te los acabo de cuero.

I'm going to make you your underwear
Like the ones the ranch hands use.
I will begin them with wool,
I will finish them with cowhide

Nunca te fíes de promesas
Ni mucho menos de amores,
Que sí te dan calabazas
Verás lo qué son ardores.

Never trust in promises,
Much less in loved ones,
Because if they give you a beating
You'll know what pain is all about.

Pon muy atento el oido
Cuando rechine la puerta;
Hay muertos que
*   no hacen ruido.*
Y son muy gordas
*   sus peñas.*

Pay close attention (a close ear)
When the door squeaks;
There are dead people
    who don't make a sound.
And the sound of the very fat
    will be your pain.

El Rey

Corrido Lento Vals   E⁷

Jose A. Jimenez

Yo sé bién que es-toy a - fue-ra pe ro el día que yo me mue-ra sé que ten - drás que llo-

rar, Llo-rar y llo - rar, Llo-rar y llo - rar; di - rás que no me qui-

sis - te pe - ro vas a es - tar muy tris - te y a - sí te vas a que-

dar._____ Con di -

ne - ro y sin di - ne - ro ha-go siem - pre lo qué quie-ro,_____

_____ y mi pa - la-bra es la ley._____

No ten - go tro - no ni rei - na,_____ ni na - die que me com-

pren - da_____ pe - ro si - go sien - do el rey_____

El Rey

Jimenez

Spanish Lyrics	English Translation

Yo sé bién que estoy afuera
Pero el día que yo me muera
Sé que tendras que llorar.
Coro: *Llorar y llorar; Llorar y llorar.*

I know well that I'm going away
But the day that I die
I know that you'll cry.
Chorus: Cry and cry; Cry and cry.

Dirás que no me quisiste
Pero vas a estar muy triste
Y así te vas a quedar.
Coro: *Llorar y llorar; Llorar y llorar.*

You know that you never loved me
But you're going to be very sad
And that's how you're going to stay.
Chorus: Cry and cry; Cry and cry.

Con dinero y sin dinero
Hago siempre lo qué quiero
Y mi palabra es la ley.
No tengo trono ni reina
Ni nadie que me comprenda
Pero sigo siendo el rey.

With money and without money
I always do what I please
And my word is the law.
I don't have a throne nor a queen
And nobody that understands me
But I continue to be the king.

Una piedra en el camino
Me enseño que mi destino
Era rodar y rodar.
Coro: *Rodar y rodar; Rodar y rodar*

A rock in the road
Showed me that my destiny
Was to roll and roll.
Chorus: Roll and roll; Roll and roll

Y después me dijo un arriero
Que no hay que llegar primero...
Pero hay que saber llegar.
Coro: *Rodar y rodar; Rodar y rodar*

And after a mule driver told me
"You may not get there first...
But you have to know how to get there."
Chorus: Roll and roll; Roll and roll

Con dinero y sin dinero
Hago siempre lo qué quiero
Y mi palabra es la ley.
No tengo trono ni reina
Ni nadie que me comprenda
Pero sigo siendo el rey.

With money and without money
I always do what I please
And my word is the law.
I don't have a throne or a queen
And no one that understands me,
But I continue to be the king.

Ella

Me can - sé de ro - gar - le, me can - sé de de - cir - le que yo sin e - lla de pe - ña mue - ro, ya no qui - so es - cu - char - me, y sus la - bios se a - brie - ron pa - ra de - cir - me: !Ya no te quie - ro! Yo sen - tí que mi vi - da se per - dia en un a - bis - mo pro - fun - do y ne - gro co - mo mi suer - te. Qui - se ha - llar el ol - vi - do al es - ti - lo Ja - lis - co, pe - ro a - que - llos ma - ria - chis y a - quel te - qui - la me hi - cie - ron llo - rar. Me can - mor.

Ella

Jiminez

Spanish Lyrics	English Translation
Me cansé de rogarle.	I got tired of begging.
Me cansé de decirle que yo	I got tired of saying that I am
sin ella.	without her.
De peña muero.	The pain is killing me.
Ya no quiso escucharme.	Already you don't want to listen to me.
Y sus labios se abrieron	And your lips know to open when
Para decirme:	They are going to say to me:
¡Ya no te quiero!	"Already, I don't want you!"
Yo sentí que mí vida se perdia	I feel that my life is falling
en un abismo,	into an abyss,
Profundo y negro. Como mi suerte.	Deep and black. Look at my fate.
Quise hallar el olvido al estilo Jalisco,	You want to find oblivion Jalisco style,
Pero aquellos mariachis	But these *mariachis*
Y aquel tequila me hicieron llorar.	And that *tequila* have me crying.
Me cansé de rogarle	I get tired of begging
con el llanto en mis ojos.	with tears in my eyes.
Alse mí copa	I pick up my cup
Y brinde con ella.	And make a toast to her.
No podia despreciarme	I can't underestimate
Era el ultimo brindis,	Making the final toast,
De un bohemio. Con una reina.	A bohemian. To a queen.
Los mariachis calliaron,	The wandering *mariachis,*
De mis manos sin fuerza	My hands are not strong enough
Cayo mi copa, sin darme cuenta.	To hold my cup *and* pay the bill.
Ella quiso quedarse	She wants to stay
cuando vio mi tristeza;	until my sadness passes;
Pero ya estaba escrito	But already it is written that
Que aquella noche perdiera su amor.	Those nights are lost to your love.

Gema

Luis Cisneros

Bolero

Tu co - mo pie - dra pre - cio - sa,_____ co - mo di - vi - na

jo - ya,__ va - lio - sa de ver - dad; si mis o - jos no me mi en ten, si mis o - jos no me en-

ga - ñan, tu be - lle - za es sin i - gual.

Tu ve u - na vez la i - lu - sión de te - ner un a - mor que me hi - cie - ra va - ler,____

lue - go que te vi mu - jer, yo te pu - de que - rer con to - di - ti - ta mi al - ma;

E - res la ge - ma que Dios con - vir - tie - ra en mu - jer pa - ra bien de mi vi - da;

por e - so quie - ro can - tar y gri - tar que te quie - ro, mu - jer con - sen - ti - da

Por e - so e - le - vo mi voz ben - di - cien - do tu nom - bre y pi - dien - do te a-

mor. mor.____

Gema

Spanish Lyrics	English Translation

Tu como piedra preciosa,
Como divina joya,
Valiosa de verdad.

You're like a precious stone,
Like a divine jewel,
Truly valuable.

Si mis ojos no me mienten,
Si mis ojos no me engañan,
Tu belleza es sin igual.

If my eyes do not lie to me,
If my eyes do not deceive me,
Your beauty is without equal.

Tu ve una vez la ilusión
De tener un amor, que me,
Hiciera valer.

I once had an illusion
That to have a love, for me,
Would make it all worthwhile.

Luego que te vi, mujer,
Yo te pude querer
Con toditita mi alma.

As soon as I saw you, woman,
I knew that I wanted you
With all my soul.

Eres la gema que Dios
Convirtiera en mujer
Para bien de mi vida.

You are the gem that God
Turned into a woman
For the good of my life.

Por eso quiero cantar
Y gritar que te quiero,
Mujer consentida.

For that reason I want to sing
And shout that I want you,
Pampered woman.

Por eso elevo mi voz,
Bendiciendo tu nombre,
Y pidiendo te amor.

For that reason I raise my voice,
Blessing your name,
And asking you for your love.

Granada

Fantasia Española

Agustin Lara

na - da___ tie-rra so - ña-da por mi,___ mi can- tar_ se vuel-ve gi - ta - no cuan-do es pa-ra

ti;___ mi can- tar___ he-cho de fan-ta- sí - a___ mi can-tar___ flor de me-

lan-co-lí-a_ que yo te ven-go a dar.___ Gra-

Gra - na-da tie rra en-san-gren-ta-da en tar-des de to-ros.___

Mu - jer que con-ser-va_el em-bru-jo de los o - jos mo - ros.___

Te sue-ño re - bel-de_y gi - ta - na cu-bier-ta de flo - res.___

— y be-so tu bo-ca de gra-na___ ju-go-sa man-za-na que_me_ha-bla de_a - mo-___

res.___ Gra-   de ro - sas de sua-ve fra-gan-cia que le die-ran

mar-co_a la Vir-gen Mo - re - na.___ Gra-na-da tu tie-rra_es-tá lle-na___ de

lin-das mu - je - res_ de san-gre_y de sol.___

Granada

Spanish Lyrics	English Translation
Granada, tierra soñada por mi,	*Granada,* my homeland,
Mí cantar se vuelve	You sing to me of returning
Gitano cuando es para ti.	When the gypsy sings to you.
Mi cantar hecho	My song is created
de fantasia,	from my imagination,
Mi cantar flor de melancolía,	My song is a melancholy flower,
Que yo te vengo a dar.	I have to go back to you.
Granada, tierra ensangrentada	*Granada,* blood-covered land
En tardes re toros.	In the afternoon of the bulls.
Mujer, que conserva el embrujo	Woman, that preserves the vision
De los ojos moros.	Of the Moorish eyes.
Te sueño rebelde	You fight sleep
Y gitana cubierta	And the gypsy woman wrapped
de flores,	in flowers,
Y beso tu boca de grana.	And I kiss your ripe mouth.
Jugosa manzana que me hable de amores	Apple juice that speaks to me of love.
De rosas de suave fragrencia	The rich aroma of roses
Que le die ran marco	That gave the mark
A la Virgen Morena.	Of the Dark Virgin.
Granada, tu tierra está llena,	*Granada,* you are the land of plenty,
De lindas mujeres de sangre y de sol.	Of beautiful women and sunsets.

Guadalajara

Guadalajara

Guizar

Spanish Lyrics	English Translation

Guadalajara, Guadalajara;
Guadalajara, Guadalajara;
Tienes el alma de provinciana,
Hueles a limpio
  rosa temprana;
A verde jara fresca del rio;
Son mil palomas,
  tu caserío.
Guadalajara, Guadalajara,
Sabes a pura tierra mojada.

¡Ay!, Colomitos lejanos.
¡Ay!, Ojitos de agua, hermanos.
¡Ay!,Colomitos inolvidables,
Inolvidables como las tardes
En que la lluvia desde la loma
Ir nos hacía hasta Zapopan.

¡Ay, Tlaquepaque pueblito!
Sus olorosos jarritos
Hacen más fresco el dulce, tepache
Para la birria, junto al mariachi,
Que en los parianes y alfarerias
Sueña con
  triste melancolía.

¡Ay!, ¡ay!, ¡ay!, ¡ay!, ¡ay!
¡Ay!,¡ay!, ¡ay!, ¡ay!, ¡ay!

Guadalajara, Guadalajara;
Guadalajara, Guadalajara;
You have the soul of the provincial.
The aroma of a just-bloomed, clean,
  pink rose.
And the fresh, green, rock-roses of the river;
There are a thousand doves,
  in your country home.
Guadalajara, Guadalajara,
You know the aroma of the pure, wet, earth.

Oh, distant, little *Colomos* Park.
Oh, sounds of the running water, brother.
Oh, unforgettable *Colomos* Park,
Unforgettable like the afternoons
In which the rain from the hill
Did not let us travel to *Zapopan.*

Oh, little town of *Tlaquepaque!*
Your sweet-smelling pots
That cooked the fresh-made candy, *tepache,*
For the goat stew, next to the *mariachi,*
That in the mall and the pottery makers' shops
I dream of these with sad,
  melancholy memories.

Oh!, oh!, oh!, oh!, oh!
Oh!, oh!, oh!, oh!, oh!

Guantanamera

Music adaptation by Pete Seeger
Lyric adaptation by Hector Argulo
based on a poem by Jose Marti

Guan-ta-na-mer- a, gua-ji-ra Guan-ta-na-mer- a.

Guan-ta-na- mer - a, gua-ji-ra Guan-ta-na-mer - a. Yo soy un

hom-bre sin-ce- ro, de don-de cre-ce la__ pal- ma,__ Yo soy un

hom-bre sin-ce- ro, de don-de cre - ce la pal- ma,__ Y an-tes

de mor - rir-me quiero, E-char mis ver-sos del al - ma.

Guan - ta - na-mer- a, gua-ji - ra Guan - ta - na-mer- a.

Guan - ta - na-mer - a gua-ji - ra Guan - ta - na-mer -

1.2.
a

3.
a Mi ver-so - a.

80

Guantanamera   *Argulo-Marti*

Spanish Lyrics	English Translation

Guantanamera, guajira,
   guantanamera.
Guantanamera, guajira
   guantanamera.
	Lady of Guantanamo, young woman,
	   lady of Guantanamo.
	Lady of Guantanamo, young woman,
	   lady of Guantanamo.

Yo soy un hombre sincero *De donde crece la palma,* *Yo soy un hombre sincero* *De donde crece la palma,* *Y antes de morrirme quiero,* *Echar mis versos alma.*	I am a sincere man From the land of the palms, I am a sincere man From the land of the palms, And before I die I wish to pour forth the poems of my soul.

Guantanamera, guajira,
   guantanamera.
Guantanamera, guajira,
   guantanamera.
	Lady of Guantanamo, young woman,
	   lady of Guantanamo.
	Lady of Guantanamo, young woman,
	   lady of Guantanamo.

Inolvidable

Bolero

Julio Gutierrez

En la vi-da hay a mo-res que nun-ca pue-den ol-vi-dar - se,____ im-bo-

rra-bles mo-men-tos que siem-pre guar-da el co-ra - zón,____ por-que a-

que-llo que un dí - a nos hi-zo tem-blar de a-le - grí - a,____ es men-

ti - ra que hoy pue-da ol-vi-dar - se con un nue-vo a- mor.____ He be-

sa-do o-tras bo-cas bus-can-do nue-vas an-sie-da - des____ y o-tros

bra-zos ex-tra - ños me es-tre-char lle-nos de e-mo- ción,____ pe-ro

só-lo con-si-guen ha-cer-me re-cor-dar los tu - yos,____ que i-nol-vi-

1.
da - ble- men-te vi-vi-rán en mí____ En la

2.
rán en mí____

82

Inolvidable

Gutierrez

Spanish Lyrics	English Translation
En la vida hay amores	In a life of loves
Que nunca pueden olvidarse,	That never can be forgotten,
Imborrables momentos	Indelible moments
Que siempre guarda el corazón.	Forever guard the heart.
Porque aquello que un día	Because that one day
Nos hizo temblar de alegría,	Will shake the happiness,
Es mentira que hoy pueda olivadarse	The lie that can be forgotten
Con un nuevo amor.	With a new love.
He besado otras bocas	I kissed other mouths
Buscando nuevas ansiedades	Searching for new yearnings
Y otros brazos extraños	I was held in other's arms
Me estrechar llenos	That embraced and filled me
* de emoción.*	with emotion.
Pero sólo consiguen hacerme	But only one could have
Recordar los tuyos,	Reminded me of yours,
Que inolvidablemente vivirán en mí.	That are unforgettable to me.

Jarabe Tapatío

Traditional (Anon.)

Son

Jarabe Tapatío

Anon.

(Our thanks to the late, great ethnomusicologist, Frances Toor, for the
following information on *jarabes*, in general, and *Jarabe Tapatío*, in particular.)

Jarabe means a syrup or sweet drink in Spanish. One dance, called *pan de jarabe*
(or sweet bread) was brought to the notice of the Inquisition as being indecent.
About the middle of the eighteenth century, dance songs were also called *sones*;
the literal meaning of *son* is "an agreeable sound."

The *Jarabe Tapatío* is the Mexican national folk dance, which developed around 1920
in Guadalajara. *Tapatío* is applied to anything from that state; hence, the name that
distinguishes it from all other *jarabes*. The *Jarabe Tapatío* is internationally known;
the famous Russian ballerina, Pavlova, learned and danced it during her visit to Mexico.

The *Jarabe Tapatío* is danced in theaters, cabarets, at secular fiestas, rodeos-actually
no program is complete without it. When it is danced by rancheros, it is even gayer
and more fiery. In many instances, a wooden platform is placed over an excavated
area or over buried jars to produce resonance. The dance sometimes lasts for hours
and much of it is improvised. The music, of course, is furnished by *mariachis*.

Jesusita

Son

Mexican Folk Song

Va-mos al bai - le y ve - rás que bo - ni - to,_____ don-de se a-

lum - bran con vien - te lin - ter - nas,_____ don - de se

bai - lan las dan - zas mo - der - nas,_____ don - de se

bai - la de mu - cho va - ci - lón._____ Y

quié - re - me Je - su - si - ta, y quié - re - me por fa - vor, y

mi - ra que soy tu a - man - te, y se - gu - ro ser - vi - dor. Va - mos al

Jesusita

Spanish Lyrics	English Translation

Vamos al baile y versa
  que bonito,
Donde se bailan las danzas modernas,
Donde se baila de mucho vacilón.
	Let's go to the dance and you'll see
	  how lovely it is
	Where they dance the modern dances,
	Where they dance with great abandon.

Coro:

Y quiéreme, Jesusita,
Y quiéreme por favor,
Y mira que soy tu amante
Y seguro servidor.

Chorus:

And love me, *Jesusita*,
And love me, please,
And see that I am your lover
And your humble servant.

Vamos al baile y versa
  que bonito,
Donde se alumbran con veinte linternas,
Donde las niñas enseñan las piernas,
Done se baile de mucho vacilón.

Let's go to the dance and you'll see
  how lovely it is
Illuminated with twenty lanterns,
Where the girls show their legs,
Where they dance with great abandon.

Jurame

Bolero

Maria Grever

To - dos di - cen que es men - ti - ra que te quie - ro, por - que
nun - ca me ha - bi - an vis - to e - na - mo - ra - da,. Yo te
ju - ro que yo mis - ma no com - pren - do el por - qué me fas - ci - na tu mi - ra - da. Cuan do es -
- toy cer - ca de ti y es - tás con - ten - to, no qui - sie - ra que de na - die te a - cor - da - ras ten - go
ce - los has - ta del pen - sa - mien - to que pue - da re - cor - dar - te a o - tra mu - jer a - ma - da.
Ju - ra - me que a un - que pa - se mu - cho tiem - po no ol - vi - da - rás el mo - men - to en que yo te co - no -
cí. Mí - ra - me, pues no hay na - da más pro - fun - do ni más gran - de en es - te
mun - do que el ca - ri - ño que te di. Bé - sa - me con un be - so e - na - mo - rado, co - mo na - die me ha be -
sa - do des - de el día en que na - cí. Quié - re - me quié - re - me has - ta la lo - cu - ra
- a - sí sa - brás la a - mar - gu - ra que es - toy su - frien - do por ti.

88

Jurame

Spanish Lyrics	English Translation
Todos dicen que es mentira *que te quiero,* *Porque nunca me habian* *visto enamorada.* *Yo te juro que yo mismo* *no comprendo* *El porqué me fascina* *tu mirada .*	Everybody says that it is a lie that I love you, Because they have never seen me in love before. I swear to you that I myself don't understand The reason why your look has fascinated me.
Cuando estoy cerca de ti y estás contento, *No quisiera que de* *nadie te acordaras.* *Tengo celos hasta del pensamiento* *Que pueda recordarte* *a otra mujer amada.*	When I am near you and I'm happy, I wish that you would remember no one else. I'm jealous of the thought That I would even remind you of another woman.
Júrame que aunque pase *mucho tiempo* *No olvidarás el momento* *en que yo te conocí.* *Mírame, pues no hay nada* *más profundo* *Ni más grande en este mundo* *Que el cariño que te di.*	Swear to me that even though much time passes You will not forget the moment we met. Look at me...there is nothing more profound Nor greater in this world Than the love that I gave you.
Bésame, con un beso enamorado *Como nadie me ha besado,* *Desde el día en que nací.*	Kiss me, with a loving kiss Like no one else has ever kissed you, Since the day I was born.
Quiéreme, quiéreme, *hasta la locura.* *Así sabrás, la amargura* *Que estoy sufriendo por ti.*	Love me, love me, until we are going mad. That way you will know the bitterness That I am suffering for you.

La Adelita

90

La Adelita

Spanish Lyrics	English Translation

En lo alto de la abrupta serranía
On the heights of an abrupt ridge,
Acampadose en contraba un regimiento,
Where a regiment was camping.
Y una moza que valiente lo seguía
A valiant young girl followed it
Locamente enamorada del sargento.
Because she was in love with a sergeant.
Popular entre la tropa era Adelita,
Favorite among the troops was Adelita,
La mujer que el sargento idolatrada
The woman idolized by the sergeant,
Porque a más de ser valiente era bonita
Because besides being brave she was pretty,
Que hasta el mismo coronel la respetaba.
And even the Colonel respected her.
Y se oia que decia aquel que canto la quería:
And it is told he said how much he loved her:

Que si Adelita se fuera con otro
If Adelita were to go with another,
Le seguiría por tierra y por mar.
He would follow her over land and sea.
Si por mar en un buque de guerra,
If by sea, in a war boat,
Si por tierra en un tren militar
If by land, in a military train.
Si Adelita ha de ser mi esposa,
Yes, Adelita must be my wife,
Si Ade;ita ha de ser mi mujer,
Yes, Adelita must be my woman.
Adelita, Adelita del alma,
Adelita, Adelita of my soul,
Adelita de mi corazón.
Adelita of my heart.

Si Adelita quisera ser mi esposa,
If Adelita wished to be my wife,
Si Adelita fuera mi mujer,
If Adelita were my woman,
Le compraria un vestido de seda,
I would buy her a silk dress,
Para llevarla a bailar al cuartel.
To take her to dance at the barracks.
Adelita, por Dios te lo ruego,
Adelita, for God's sake I beg you
Calma el fuego de esta mi pasión,
To calm the fire of this my passion,
Porque te amo y te quiero rendido
Because I adore you and love you devotedly
Y por ti sufre mi fiel corazon.
And for you my faithful heart suffers.

Toca el clarin de campaña a la guerra,
The bugle of battle plays to war,
Sale el valienta guerrero a pelear,
The brave knight leaves to fight,
Correrán los arroyos de sangre,
Streams of blood shall flow,
¡Que gobierne un tirano jamás!
Let no tyrant ever govern!
Y si acaso yo muero en campaña
And if perchance I die in battle
Y mi cuerpo en la sierra va a quedar,
And my body remains in the sierra,
Adelita, por Dios te lo ruego,
Adelita, for God's sake I beg you,
Con tus ojos me vas a llorar.
To weep for me with your eyes.

La Bamba

Mexican Folk Song

La Bamba   *Anon*

Spanish Lyrics	English Translation

Para bailar la bamba,

Para bailar la bamba se necesita

Una poca de gracia,

Una poca de gracia y otro cosita.

Ay! arriba y arriba, Y arriba y arriba, arriba iré.

To dance the bamba,

To dance the bamba you need

A little bit of grace,

A little bit of grace and another little thing.

Oh! up and up, And up, and up, up I'll go.

Yo no soy marinero,

Yo no soy marinero, por ti seré,

Por ti seré, por ti seré.

(Coro) Bamba, bamba, bamba!...(etc.)

I'm not a sailor,

I'm not a sailor, but for you I'll be one,

For you I'll be one, for you I'll be one.

(Chorus) Bamba, bamba, bamba!...(etc.)

Para subir al cielo se necesita

Una escalera grande.

Una escalera grande y otra chiquita.

Ay!, arriba y arriba, Y arriba y arriba, arriba iré...

To go up to heaven you'll need

A big ladder

A big ladder and another small thing.

Oh, up and up, And up and up, up I'll go...

Yo no soy marinero,

Yo no soy marinero, soy capitán,

Soy capitán, soy capitán.

(Coro) Bamba, bamba, bamba!...(etc.)

I'm not a sailor,

I'm not a sailor, I'm a captain,

I'm a captain, I'm a captain.

(Chorus) Bamba, bamba, bamba!...(etc.)

Una vez que te dije,

Una vez que te dije que era bonita,

Se te puso la cara,

Se te puso la cara coloradita,

Ay!, arriba y arriba, Y arriba y arriba, arriba iré...

Once I told you,

Once I told you that you were pretty,

And you blushed,

And your face turned a little red,

Oh, up and up, And up and up, up I'll go...

Una vez que te dije,

Una vez que te dije que era muy guapo.

Se te puso la cara,

Se te puso la cara color de sapo.

Ay!, arriba y arriba, Y arriba y arriba, arriba iré...

(There are hundreds of verses to this song.

Every verse is double entendre.)

Once I told you,

Once I told you that you were very handsome.

And your face turned,

And your face turned the color of a toad.

Oh, up and up, And up and up, up I'll go...

(The above are the most common verses.

These are rated more "PG" than "X")

La Cucaracha

Revolutionary Song from Chihuahua

La cu - ca - ra - cha, la cu - ca - ra - cha

ya no pue - de ca - mi - nar___ por-que no tie - ne, por-que la fal - ta

ma - ri - jua - na que fu - mar___ la cu - ca ra - cha.

1. ya mu - rió la cu - ca - ra - cha   ya la lle - vana en - te - rrar
2. con las bar - bas de Ca - rran - za   voy a ha - cer una to - quilla,

en - tre cua - tro zo - pi - lo - tes   y un ra - tón de sa - cris - tan.
Pá pon - ér - sel a al som - bre - ro   de su pad - re Pan cho Villa.

La Cucaracha

Anon

Spanish Lyrics	English Translation
La cucaracha, la cucaracha,	The cockroach, the cockroach,
Ya no puede caminar;	He can't walk anymore;
Porque no tiene, porque la falta	Because he doesn't have (because he lacks)
Marijuana que fumar.	Marijuana to smoke.
Ya murió la cucaracha,	The cockroach is already dead,
Ya la llevan a enterrar,	And they take it to bury,
Entre cuatro zopilotes	Between four buzzards
Y un ratón de sacristan.	And a sacred rat.
Con las barbas de Carranza,	By the beard of *Carranza*,
Voy a hacer una toquilla,	I'm going to have a toke,
Pa' ponérsela al sombrero	I'll put it in the hat
De su padre, Pancho Villa.	Of your father, *Pancho Villa*.
Un panadero fue a misa,	A baker went to mass,
No encontrando que rezar	Not knowing how to pray
Le pidio a la Virgen pura,	To the pure Virgin Mary,
Marijuana pa' fumar.	For marijuana to smoke.
Una cosa me da risa:	One thing that makes me laugh:
Pancho Villa sin camisa;	*Pancho Villa* without a shirt;
Ya se van los carrancistas	And when the supporters of *Carranza* go
Porque vienen	Then the supporters of
* los villistas.*	*Pancho Villa* will come.
Para sarapes, Saltillo;	For blankets, *Saltillo* is the best place;
Chihuahua para soldados;	For soldiers, *Chihuahua*;
Para mujeres, Jalisco;	For women, *Jalisco*;
Para amar, toditos lados.	For love, all sides (anywhere & everywhere).

La Feria de las Flores

Vals — Chucho Monge

Me gus - ta can - tar - le al vien - to por - que vue - lan mis can - ta - res,___ y di - go lo qué yo sien - to___ ___ en to - di - tos los lu - gar - es.___ A - quí vi - ne por - que vi - ne___ a la fe - ria de las flo - res,___ no hay ce - rro que se me em - pi - ne___ ni cua - co que se me a to - re.___ re.

La Feria de las Flores   *Monge*

Spanish Lyrics	English Translation
Me gusta cantarle al viento	I like to sing to the wind
Porque vuelan mis cantares,	Because my songs fly,
Y digo lo qué yo siento	And I say what I feel
En toditos los lugares	Everywhere.
Aquí vine porque vine	I came here to go
A la feria de las flores.	To the flower market.
No hay cerro que se me empine	There is no hill that will slow me down,
Ni cuaco que se me atore.	Nor will a scrawny horse stop me.
En mí caballo retinto	On my dark horse
He venido de muy lejos,	I've come from far away,
Y traigo pistola al cinto	And I have a gun in my belt.
Y con ella doy consejos.	And with her (the gun) I give advice.
Atraversé la montaña	I crossed the mountains
Pa' venir a ver las flores.	To come and see the flowers.
Aquí hay una rosa huraña,	Here, there is one unsociable rose,
Que es la flor de mis amores.	That is the flower of my love.
Y aunque otro "quera"	And although another wants
cortarla	to cut (pick) her
Yo la "devise" primero.	It was I who saw her first.
Y juro que he de robarla,	And I swear I'm going to steal her,
Aunque tenga jardinero.	Even though there is a gardener.
Yo la he de ver transplantada	I'm going to see her transplanted
En el huerto de mi casa	In the garden of my house
Y si sale el jardinero,	And if the gardener comes out,
Pos a ver...a ver	Well, let's see...let's see
qué pasa.	what happens.

Las Alteñitas

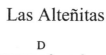

Corrido

Juan Jose Espinosa

Va - mos a Te - pa, tie - rra so - ña - da, don - de la vi - da_es un pri - mor;_____ a - llá me_es - pe - ra ni cha - pe - tea - da, la ú - ni - ca due - ña de mi_a - mor._____ Es - tan bo - ni - ta, mi cha pa - rri - ta, qué cuan - do va_al tem - plo_a re - zar,_____ to dos la lla - man_____ la vir - gen - ci - ta_____ de la bo - qui - ta de co - ral._____ Qué lin das las ma - ña nas cuan - do sa - le_el sol, a - sí son las Al - te - ñas de_és - te al - re - de - dor A - le - gres y bo - ni - tas to do_el tiem - po_es - tán, las lin - das Al - te - ñi - tas de Te - pa - ti - tlán. _____

Las Alteñitas

Espinoza

Spanish Lyrics	English Translation

Vamos a Tepa,
Tierra soñada,
Donde la vida es un primor.
Allá me espera
Mí chapeteada,
La única dueña de mi amor.

Lets go to *Tepa,*
Land of my dreams,
Where life is beautiful.
There awaits me
My rosy-cheeked (little girl),
The only owner of my love.

Estan bonita,
Mi chaparrita,
Que cuando va al templo a rezar,
Todos la llaman
La virgencíta
De la boquita de coral.

She's so beautiful,
My little "shorty,"
That when she goes to the temple to pray,
Everybody calls her
The little virgin
With the little coral mouth.

Qué lindas las mañanas
Cuando sale el sol.
Si son las Alteñas
* de éste alrededor.*
Alegres y bonitas
Todo el tiempo están,
Las lindas Alteñitas de Tepatitlán.

How beautiful are the mornings
When the sun rises.
That's how the *Alteñas* are
  in these surroundings.
Happy and pretty
They are, all of the time,
The beautiful *Alteñitas* of *Tepatitlán.*

Las Mañanitas

Traditional Mexican Birthday Song

Vals

Es-tas son las ma - ña- ni tas que can - ta ba el Rey Da-

vid; hoy por ser día de tu san - to te las can - ta - mos a

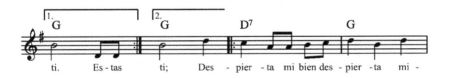

ti. Es - tas ti; Des - pier -ta mi bien des - pier -ta mi -

ra que ya a - ma -ne - ció ya los pa - ja - ri - tos

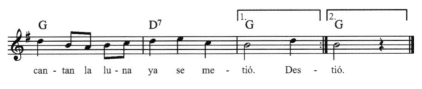

can - tan la lu - na ya se me - tió. Des - tió.

Las Mañanitas

Spanish Lyrics	English Translation
Estas son las mañanitas,	These are the morning songs,
Que cantaba el Rey David;	That King David used to sing;
Hoy por ser día de tu santo	Because today is your holy patron's day,
Te las cantamos a ti.	We all sing to you..
Despierta, mi bien, despierta,	Wake up, my good friend, wake up,
Mira, que ya amaneció,	Look, day has dawned,
Ya los pajaritos cantan,	Now the little birds are singing,
La luna ya se metió.	The moon has disappeared.
Quisiera ser solecito,	It wanted
Para entrar por tu ventana	To enter through your window
Y darte los buenos dias,	And deliver a great day to you
Acostadito en tu cama.	While you were lying in your bed.
Por la luna doy un peso,	For the moon, I'll give you a dollar,
Por el sol doy un toston,	For the sun, I'll give you a fifty cent piece,
Por mí amiga, Marianita,	For my friend, little Marian,
La vida y el corazón.	My life and my heart.
De las estrellas del cielo,	Of all the stars in the sky,
Quisiera bajarte dos,	I want two of the lower ones
	(the ones that I can touch),
Y otra para decirte adios.	And the other for saying goodbye.

Note: This is the Mexican equivalent of "Happy Birthday to You."

When sung for women, the words *"a las muchachas bonitas"* are substituted for *"hoy por ser dia de tu santo,"* which means "because it is your holy patron's day" and, in the next verse, the words *"mi bien"* are replaced by the name of the person being honored.

Usually only the first two verses are played and sung to honor the person celebrating his or her birthday.

Llorarás, Llorarás

Bolero

Rafael Ramirez

102

Llororás, Llororás

Spanish Lyrics	English Translation
Llorarás, llorarás	You will weep, you will weep
Mí partida,	At my departure,
Aunque quieras arrancarme	Even though you want to tear me out
De tu ser.	Of your life.
Cuando sientas el calor	When you feel the heat
De otras caricias,	Of other caresses,
Mí receuerdo ha de brillar	My memory will shine
Donde tu estés.	Wherever you are.
Has de ver que mi amor	You will see that my love
Fue sincero,	Was sincere,
Y que nunca comprendiste	And that you never understood
Mí penar.	My sorrow.
Cuando sientas	When you feel
La nostalgia	The nostalgia
Por mis besos	For my kisses
Llorarás, llorarás, llorarás.	You will weep, weep, weep.
Has de ver que mi amor	You will see that my love
Fue sincero,	Was sincere,
Y que nunca comprendiste	And that you never understood
Mí penar.	My sorrow.
Cuando sientas	When you feel
La nostalgia	The nostalgia
Por mis besos,	For my kisses,
Llorarás, llorarás, llorarás.	You will weep, weep, weep.

Madrid

Agustin Lara

Shottis

104

Madrid

Spanish Lyrics	English Translation
Cuando llegues a Madrid, chulona mia,	When you go to Madrid, my precious one,
Voy a hacerte	I'm going to make you an empress
Emperatriz de lavapiés;	by washing your feet;
Y al alfombrarte con claveles	And carnations cover you
la Gran Via,	on the Grand Boulevard,
Y a bañarte con víníllo de Jerez.	And you will be bathed in sherry wine.
En Chicote un agasajo postinero,	You'll be whipped at a swanky banquet,
Con la crema de la intelectualidad,	With the cream of intellectuality,
Y la gracia de un piropo retrechercho	And the grace of flirtatious, crafty remarks
Más castizo que la calle de Alcalá	More pure than the streets of *Alcalá.*
Madrid, Madrid, Madrid,	Madrid, Madrid, Madrid,
Pedazo de la España en que naci,	A piece of the Spain in which I was born,
Por algo to hizo Díos	There is a reason why God made you
La cuña del requiebro	The cradle of compliments
y del Schottis.	and popular European dance.
Madrid, Madrid, Madrid,	Madrid, Madrid, Madrid,
En México se piensa mucho en tí,	In *Mexico* they think highly of you,
Por el sabor que tienen tus verbenas,	For the flavor of your evening parties,
Por tantas cosas buenas	For so many good things
Que soñamos desde aquí.	That we dream of from here.
Y vas averlo qué es canela fina,	Now you're going to see what it is like
Y armar la tremolina	And to create an uproar
Cuando llegues a Madrid.	When you arrive in Madrid.

Maria Elena

Maria Elena

Spanish Lyrics	English Translation
¡Tuyo es mi corazón,	My heart is yours,
O, sol de mi querer,	Oh, sun of my wishes,
Mujer de mi ilusión,	Woman of my dreams,
Mi amor te con sagré!	My love to whom I am dedicated!
Mi vida la embellece	My life is made beautiful by
Una esperanza azul,	One blue hope,
Mi vida tiene un cielo	My life has a sky
Que le diste tu.	That is far away.
¡Tuyo es mi corazón,	My heart is yours,
O, sol de mi querer,	Oh, sun of my wishes,
Tuyo es todo mi ser,	You are everything to me,
Tuyo es, mujer!	You are, woman!
Ya todo	Already you are everything
* el corazón*	to my heart
Te los entregué.	To you I surrender.
¡Eres mi fé,	You are my faith,
Eres mi Díos	You are my God,
Eres mi amor!	You are my love!
¡Tuyo es mi corazón,	My heart is yours,
Mi amor!	My love!

México Lindo

Moderato — Chucho Monge

Voz de la gui - ta - rra mi - a,_____ al des - per -
tar la ma - ña - na,_____ quie - ro can - tar la - le -
grí - a_____ de mi tie - rra mé - xi - ca - na._____
del a - mor de_____ mis a - mo - res._____
Mé - xi - co lin - do y que - ri - do, si mue - ro le - jos de ti,_____
que di - gan que es - toy dor - mi - do y que me trai - gan a - quí._____
Que di - gan que es - toy dor - mi - do y que me
trai - gan a - quí,_____ Mé - xi - co lin - do y que - ri
do, si mue - ro le -_____ jos de ti._____

México Lindo

Spanish Lyrics	English Translation
Voz de la guitarra mia,	Voice of my guitar,
Al despertar la mañana,	When the morning awakens,
Quiero cantar la alegria	I want to sing of the happiness
De mi tierra méxicana.	Of my Mexican homeland.
Yo le canto a sus volcanes,	I want to sing of her volcanoes,
A sus praderas y flores,	And her prairies and flowers,
Que son como talismanes	That are as talismans
Del amor de mi amores.	Of the love of my loves.
México lindo y querido,	Beautiful and dear *México*,
Si muero lejos de ti,	If I die far from you,
Que digan que estoy dormido	Let them say that I'm asleep
Y que me traigan aquí.	And let them bring me home.
Que digan que estoy dormido	Let them say that I'm asleep
Y que me traigan aquí.	And let them bring me home.
México lindo y querido,	Beautiful and dear *México*,
Si muero lejos de ti.	If I die far from you.
Que me entierren	Let them bury me
en la sierra,	in the mountain range,
Al pie de los magueyales	At the foot of the agaves
Y que me cubra la tierra,	And let the earth cover me,
Que es cuña de hombre cabales.	Which is the cradle of honorable men.
Voz de la guitarra mia,	Voice of my guitar,
Al despertar la mañana,	When the morning awakens,
Quiero cantar la alegria	I want to sing of the happiness
De mi tierra méxicana.	Of my Mexican homeland.

Mi Ranchito

A - llá al pie de la mon - ta - ña, don - de tem - pra - no se o - cul - ta el sol,___ que - do mi ran - chi - to tris - te y a - ban - do - na - da ya mi la - bor.___ A - llí me pa - sé los a - ños y me en - con - tré mi pri - mer a - mor,___ y fue - ron los de - sen - ga - ños los que ma - ta - ron ya mi i - lu - sión___ Ay,___ co - ra - zón, que te vas, pa - ra nun - ca vol - ver,___ no me di - gas a - diós___ no___ te des - pi - das ja - más, si no quie - res sa - ber___ de la au - sen - cia el do - lor.___ Ay,___ co - ra - zón que te vas pa - ra nun - ca vol - ver,___ no me di - gas a - diós,___ vuel -___ ve a - le - grar con tu a - mor al ran - chi - to que fue___ en mi vi - da i - lu - sión.___

Mi Ranchito

Spanish Lyrics	English Translation
Allá al pie *de la montaña,* *Donde temprano se oculta el sol,* *Quedo mi ranchito triste* *Y abandonada ya mi labor.*	There, at the foot of the mountain, Where the sun sets early, I stayed at my little ranch And abandoned my work.
Allí me pasé los años *Y me encontré mi primer amor* *Y fueron* *los desengaños,* *Los que mataron ya mí ilusión.*	There I passed the years And found my first love And experienced the disappointments, The ones that killed my illusions.
Ay, corazón, que te vas, *Para nunca volver.* *No me digas adiós,* *No te despidas jamás,* *Si no quieres saber* *De la ausencia el dolor.*	Oh, my heart, you left me, Never to return. Don't tell me goodbye, Never say "farewell" to me, If you don't want to know Of the pain of loss.
Ay, corazón que te vas, *Para nunca volver.* *No me digas adiós,* *Vuelve alegrar con tu amor* *Al ranchito que fue* *En mí vida ilusión.*	Oh, my heart, you left me, Never to return. Don't tell me goodbye, Return happy, with your love, To the little ranch that you left In my illusion of life.

No Volveré

Cancion Vals

Esperon - Cortazar

Cuan-do le-jos te en cuen-tres-de- mí,_____ cuan-do quie-ras que es - té yo con-

ti - go_____ no ha-lla - rás un re - cuer-do de mí_____ ni ten-

drás más a - mo - res con - mi - go_____ Yo te

ju - ro que no vol - ve - ré_____ a un - que me ha ga pe -

da - zos la vi - da:_____ si u - na vez con lo - cu - ra te a -

mé_____ ya de mi al-ma es ta - rás des - pe - di - da._____

No_____ vol-ve - ré,_____ te lo ju - ro por Dios que me mi - ra,_____ te lo

di - go llo - ran-do de ra - bia,_____ no vol - ve - ré_____

2. _____ don - de yo tu re - cuer-do a-hoga - ré._____

No Volveré

Spanish Lyrics	English Translation
Cuando lejos te encuentres de mí,	When you're far away from me,
Cuando quieros que esté yo contigo,	When you want me to be with you,
No hallarás un recuerdo de mí,	You won't have a memory of me,
Ni tendrás más amores conmigo.	You won't have any more love with me.
Yo te juro que no volveré,	I swear to you that I won't come back,
Aunque me haga pedazos la vida.	Even though life breaks me to pieces.
Si una vez con locura te amé,	If at any time I loved you madly,
Ya de mí alma estarás	Already I have dismissed you
despidida.	from my soul.
No volveré,	I won't come back,
Te lo juro por Dios que me mira.	I swear by God who looks upon me,
Te lo digo llorando de rabia,	I'm telling you in a crying rage,
No volveré.	I won't come back.
No parare hasta ver que mi llando	I won't stop until my crying
a formado	has formed
Un arroyo de olvido anegado	A river of forgotten memories
Donde yo tu	Where I will drown any
recuerdo ahogare.	memory of you.

Noche de Ronda

María Teresa Lara

No-che de Ron - da___ qué tris - te pa - sas___ qué tris - te cru - zas por mi bal - cón.___ No-che de Ron - da___ co-mo me hie - res___ co-mo las - ti - mas mi co - ra - zón.___ Lu-na que se quie - bra so - bre la ti - nie - bla de mi so - le - dad. ¿A dón - de vas? dí - me si es-ta no-che tu te vas de Ron-da co-mo e-lla se fue___ ¿con quién es - tás?___ dí - le que la quie - ro dí - le que me muer - o de tan - to es - pe - rar,___ que vuel - va ya,___ que las ron - das___ no son bue - nas, que ha - cen da - ño,___ que dan pe - ñas___ que se a - ca - ba por___ llo - rar___ Lu - na que se - rar.

114

Noche de Ronda

M.T.Lara

Spanish Lyrics	English Translation
Noche de Ronda, qué triste pasas,	Around nighttime, how sadly time passes,
Qué triste cruzas, por mí balcón.	How sadly you cross beneath my balcony.
Noche de Ronda, como me hieres,	Around nighttime, how you hurt me,
Como lastimas mí corazón.	How my heart aches.
Luna que se quiebra	The moon that breaks
Sobre la tiniebla de mi soledad,	Over the shadows of my solitude,
¿A dónde vas?	Where did you go?
Dime si esta noche	Tell me tonight if
Tu te vas de Ronda como ella	You too will go around nighttime,
se fue.	as she went away.
¿Con quién estás?	Who are you with?
Dile que la quiero,	Tell them that I want her,
Dile que me muero	Tell them that I am dying
de tanto esperar,	for hoping so much,
Que vuelva ya;	That she will come back soon;
Que las rondas no son buenas,	The nighttime is not good,
Que hacen daño, que dan peñas,	It is harmful, it causes so much pain
Que se acaba por llorar.	That I am exhausted from crying.

115

Nunca, Nunca, Nunca

Ignacio Fernandez

Nun- ca, nunca, nun - ca pen - sé que me a - ma - ras, co - mo i - ba a pen - sar - lo tan po - bre que soy. Co - mo i - ba a pen - sar - lo si e-res tan bo - ni - ta, si e - res tan her - mo - sa, si e-res tan gen - til. Su-frí mu-cho tiem-po, llo-ré mu-chas ve - ces, la vi-da in-cle-men-te to-do me ne - gó. Nun-ca me mi - ras-te co-mo aho-ra me mí-ras ben-di-to sea el cie-lo que al fin me es-cu-chó Nun-ca, nun-ca, chó. Yo ya no me a - cuer-do ni quie-ro a-cor-dar-me de tan-tas tris - te - zas y tan - to do - lor, tu a-mor y mi di-cha due-ña de mi vi - da han he-cho que ol - vi - de lo qué yo su - frí. Nun-ca, nun-ca, nun - ca, cre - í me - re - cer - te y aho-ra que e-res mi - a ya no sé qué ha - cer, y por-que e-res bue - na y por que e - res bo - ni - ta te en - tre - go los res - tos del que fue mi a- mor.____

Nunca, Nunca, Nunca   *Fernandez*

Spanish Lyrics	English Translation

Nunca, nunca, nunca pense
  que me amares.

Never, never, never did I think
  that you loved me.

Como iba a pensarlo, tan pobre que soy,

How would I ever know, I'm so poor,

Como iba a pensarlo si eres tan bonita,

How would I ever know if you're so pretty,

Si eres tan hermosa, si eres tan gentil.

Yes, you're so beautiful, yes, you're so gentle.

Sufrí mucho tiempo, lloré muchas veces,

I suffered for a long time, I cried many times,

La vida inclemente todo me negó

This harsh life denied me everything.

Nunca me miraste como
  ahora me miras,

You never looked at me like you
  look at me now,

Bendito sea el cielo que al fin me escuchó.

Blessed is the sky that finally heard me.

Nunca, nunca, nunca pense que tus labios

Never, never, never did I think that your lips

Me hicieran caricias que tanto anhele,

Would caress me as I so longed for you,

Como ibe a pensarlo si siempre que habladan

I always thought that when they spoke

Caían en mi vida, gotitas de hielo.

Drops of ice would fall on me.

Las dichas ajenas fueron
  los testigos

Different degrees of happiness were
  the witnesses

De todas las pensas que pase por ti.

Of all the pain that I went through for you.

Nunca me besaste como ahora me besas,

You never kissed me like you kiss me now,

Bendito sea el cielo que al fin me escuchó.

Blessed is the sky that finally heard me.

Yo ya no me acuerdo ni
  quiero acordarme

I no longer remember, nor do I
  want to remember,

De tantas tristezas y tanto dolor;

The sadness and the pain;

Tu amor y mi dicha,
  dueña de mí vida,

Your love and my happiness,
  the owners of my life,

Han hecho que olvide lo qué yo sufrí.

Have made me forget what I have suffered.

Nunca, nunca,
  nunca creí merecerte,

Never, never,
  never did I think I deserved you,

Y ahora que eres mia
  ya no sé qué hacer,

And now that you're mine,
  I don't know what to do,

Y porque eres buena y porque eres bonita,

And because you're so good and so pretty,

Te entrego los restos del que fue mi amor.

I give you the remainder of what was my love.

Ojos Españoles

Danza

B. Kaempfert-C. Mapel

Son_____ co - mo el mar,_____
co - mo el a - zul del cie - lo y co - mo el sol._____
Son_____ del co - lor
del cla - vel que em - pie - za a des - per - tar._____
Son_____ al - go más
que las es - tre - llas al a - no - che - cer._____
¡O_____ lé yo - lé!_____ los
o - jos de la es - pa - ño - la que yo a - mé.
Que yo a - mé_____ y que no ol - vi - da-
ré.

Ojos Españoles

Kaempfert-Mapel

Spanish Lyrics	English Translation
Son, como el mar,	They were like the sea,
Como el azul del cielo y con el sol.	Like the blue of the sky with the sun.
Son, del color	They were the color
Del clavel que empieza a despertar.	Of a carnation that begins to bloom.
Son, algo más,	And something more,
Que las estrellas al anochecer.	Like the stars at nightfall.
Olé y olé,	Bravo and bravo,
Los ojos de la española que yo amé.	The eyes of the Spanish girl that I loved.
Yo, fui feliz,	I was happy
Mirando aquellos ojos de mi amor.	Looking at her eyes, my love.
Yo, nunca vi.	I never saw
Ni en al arco iris su color.	The color of her eyes in the colors of the rainbow.
Son, algo más,	And something more,
Que las estrellas al anochecer.	Like the stars at nightfall.
Olé y olé,	Bravo and bravo,
Los ojos de la española que yo amé,	The eyes of the Spanish girl that I loved.
Ojos de amor que nunca olvidaré.	The eyes of a lover that I never will forget.

Perfidia

Alberto Dominguez

Moderato

Na-die com-pren-do lo qué su-fro yo,_ can-to, pues ya no pue-do so-llo-zar;_ so-lo tem-blan-do de an-sie-dad es-toy, to-dos me mi-ran y se van. Mu- jer____ si pue-des tú con Dios ha-blar,____ pre-gún-ta-le si yo al-gu-na vez te he de-ja-do de a-do-rar.____ Y el____ Te he bus-ca-do don-de quie-ra que yo voy, y no te pue-do ha-llar, pa-ra qué quie-ro o-tros be-sos si tus la-bios no me quie-ren ya be-sar, y tú____ quién sa-be por dón-de an-da-rás____ quién sa-be que a-ven-tu-ra ten-drás que le-jos es-tás de mí._

Perfidia

Spanish Lyrics	English Translation
Nadie comprendo lo qué sufro yo,	Nobody understands how I suffer,
Canto, pues ya no puedo sollozar,	I am on edge, and can't be alone;
Solo, temblando de ansiedad estoy,	Alone, I'm trembling with anxiety
Todos me miran y se van.	At everything that I see and do.
Mujer,	Woman,
Si puedes tú con Dios hablar,	If you could only have talked with God,
Pregúntale si yo,	If you had asked Him, if there were
alguna vez	another way
Te he dejado de adorar.	That you could have left your lover.
Y el mar,	And the sea,
Espejo de mí corazón,	The mirror of my heart,
Las veces qué me ha visto llorar	Sees how I'm crying tears at
La perfidia de tu amor.	The treachery of your love.
Te he buscado donde	That you could have searched where
Quiera que yo voy,	Ever you wanted to go,
Y no te puedo hallar,	And you weren't able to find,
¿Para qué quiero otros besos si tus	For how will I want other kisses than yours
Labios ni me quieren ya besar?	When I have kissed no one else but you?
Y tú,	And you,
Quien sabe por donde andarás,	Who knows where you give,
Quien sabe qué aventura tendrás,	Who knows how that love affair will end,
¡Qué lejos estás de mí!	That is far away from me!

Por un Amor

Andante — G — D⁷ — Gilberto Parra

Por un a-mor me des-ve-lo y vi-vo a-pa-sio-na-do por un a-mor en mi vi-da de-jó pa-ra siem-pre a-mar-go do-lor. Po-bre de mí Es-ta vi-da me-jor que se a-ca-be no es pa-ra mí, Po-bre de mí, Po-bre de mí, Cuán-to su-fre mi pe-cho que la-te tan só-lo por ti. Por un a-ti.

Por un Amor *Parra*

Spanish Lyrics	English Translation
Por un amor,	For a love,
Me desvelo y vivo apasionado;	I can't sleep and I live full of passion;
Por un amor,	I have a love
En mi vida dejó	That left in my life,
Para siempre amargo dolor.	Forever, a bitter pain.
Pobre de mí.	Poor me.
Esta vida mejor que se acabe.	This life would be better if it would end.
No es para mí.	It's not for me.
Pobre de mí,	Poor me,
(Ay, corazón,)	(Oh, my heart,)
Pobre de mí,	Poor me,
(No sufras más;)	(Don't suffer any more;)
Cuánto sufre mi pecho	How great is the suffering in my breast
Que late tan sólo por ti.	That throbs only for you.
Por un amor,	For a love,
He llorado gotitas de sangre	I cry droplets of the blood
Del corazón,	Of my heart,
Me ha dejado con el alma herida	You leave my mortally injured soul
Sin compasión.	Without any compassion.
Pobre de mi.	Poor me.
Esta vida mejor que se acabe.	This life would be better if it would end.
No es para mí.	It's not for me.
Pobre de mí,	Poor me,
(Ay, corazón,)	(Oh, my heart,)
Pobre de mí,	Poor me,
(No sufras más;)	(Don't suffer any more;)
Cuánto sufre mi pecho	How great is the suffering in my breast
Que late tan sólo por ti.	That throbs only for you.

Sabor a Mí

Alvaro Carrillo

Tan-to tiem-po dis-fru - ta-mos es-te a- mor,_____ nues-tras al-mas se a-cer ca - ron tan - to a - sí_____ que yo guar-do tu sa-bor, pe - ro tú lle - vas tam- bién sa - bor a mí; si ne-ga-ras mi pre - sen-cia en tu vi- vir_____ bas - ta - ría con a - bra - sar-te y con-ver- sar_____ tan - ta vi - da yo te di que por fuer-za tie-nes ya sa - bor a mí_____ No pre- ten - do ser tu due-ño, no soy na-da, yo no ten-go va-ni - dad; de mi vi-da doy lo bue-no, yo tan po-bre ¿Que o-tra co-sa pue-do dar? Pa-sa - rán más de mil a - ños, mu-chos más_____ yo no sé si ten-ga a - mor la e-ter - ni - dad_____ pe ro a-llá tal co-mo a - quí en la bo-ca lle-va - rás sa-bor a mí_____

Sabor a Mi

Carrillo

Spanish Lyrics	English Translation
Tanto tiempo disfrutamos este amor,	For so much time we enjoyed this love,
Nuestras almas se acercaron,	Our souls became closer,
Tanto así que yo guardo	So much so that I keep
Tu sabor...pero tú llevas también	Your taste...but you also have
Sabor a mí.	The taste of me.
Si negaras mi presencia en tu vivir,	If you deny my presence in your life,
Bastaría con abrasarte y conversar.	Hugs and conversation would be enough.
Tanta vida yo te di	So much of my life I gave to you
Que por fuerza tienes ya	That through my strength you have
sabor a mí.	the taste of me.
No pretendo ser tu dueño,	I don't pretend to be your owner,
No soy nada, yo no tengo vanidad.	I am nothing, I have no vanity.
De mi vida doy lo bueno,	I give the best of my life,
Yo tan pobre, ¿que otra cosa puedo dar?	I'm so poor, what else can I give?
Pasarán más de mil años	A thousand years could go by
muchos más...	and many more.
Yo no sé si tengo amor la eternidad...	I don't know if eternity has love,
Pero allá tal como aquí,	But there in heaven, as here on earth,
En la boca llevarás	In your mouth you'll have
sabor a mí.	the taste of me.

Siempre en Mi Corazón

Siempre en Mi Corazón *Lecuona*

Spanish Lyrics	English Translation
Siempre esta en mi corazón.	You are always in my heart.
El recuerdo de tu amor,	The memory of your love,
Que al igual que tu canción,	That is equal to your song,
Quito de mí ama su dolor.	Relieves my lady's pain.
Siempre esta en mi corazón.	You are always in my heart.
La nostalgia de tu ser,	The nostalgia of your being,
Ya hora puedo comprender.	I am now able to understand.
Que dulce ha sido tu perdón.	How sweet to have your forgiveness.
La visión de mí soñar,	The vision of my dream,
Me hizo ver con emoción,	Makes me see with emotion
Que fue tu alma inspiración,	That lights your soul's inspiration,
	Where it applies to my thirst for your
Donde aplaqué mí sed de amar.	love.
Hoy tan solo es pero verte,	Today you have only spilled it out,
Y ya nunca más	And you will never be able
perderte,	to lose it more,
Mientras tanto que tu amor,	And all the while that's your love,
Siempre esta en mi corazón.	You are always in my heart.

127

Sin Ti

128

Sin Ti

Spanish Lyrics	English Translation

Sin ti,
No podré vivir jamás.
Y pensar que nunca más
Estarás junto a mí.

Without you,
I will never be able to live.
And to think that never more
Will you be together with me.

Sin ti,
Qué me puede ya importar.
Si lo qué me hace llorar
Está lejos de aquí.

Without you,
What could matter to me?
What could certainly make me cry
Is far from here.

Sin ti,
No hay clemencia en dolor.
La esperanza de mi amor
Te la llevas al fin.

Without you,
There is no mercy in my pain.
The hope of my love
You have finally taken it.

Sin ti,
Es inútil vivir.
Como inútil será
El quererte olvidar.

Without you,
It is useless to live.
Just as useless as it will be
To try to forget you.

Solamente Una Vez

Ranking: #5   # Solamente Una Vez   *A. Lara*

Spanish Lyrics	English Translation

Solamente una vez
Ame en la vida.
Solamente una vez
Y nada más.

Only one time
I have loved in this life.
Only one time
And never more.

Una vez, nada más,
En mi huerto brillo la esperanza,
La esperanza que alumbra
El camino de mi soledad.

One time, never more,
In my orchard hope shined,
The hope that illuminates
The road of my solitude.

Una vez, nada más,
Se entrega el alma,
Con la dulce y
   total renunciación;
Y cuando ese milagro realiza
El prodigio de amarse,
Hay campanas de fiesta
Que cantan
En el corazón.

One time, never more,
You surrender your soul,
With the sweet and
   complete resignation;
And when that miracle accomplishes
The prodigy of love,
Then the bells that toll at the fiesta
Will sing
In your heart.

Somos Novios

Ranking: #11   # Somos Novios   *Manzanero*

Spanish Lyrics	English Translation

Somos novios,
Pues los dos sentimos mutuo
  amor profundo,
Y con eso ya ganamos
Lo más grande de éste mundo.

We are sweethearts,
Because we both feel mutual
  profound love,
And with that, we've already won
The greatest thing in this world.

Nos amamos, nos besamos,
Como novios nos deseamos
Y hasta a veces sin motivo,
Sin razon
  nos enojamos.

We love each other, we kiss each other,
As sweethearts we desire each other,
And sometimes, without any motive,
Without any reason,
  we get angry at each other.

Somos novios,
Mantenemos un cariño limpio y puro.
Como todos, procuramos
El momento más obscuro
Para hablamos,
Para darmos el más dulce
  de los besos.

We are sweethearts,
We maintain a love clean and pure.
Like everyone else, we seek
A dark, secluded moment
To speak to each other,
To give each other the sweetest
  of kisses.

Recordar de qué
  color son los cerezos,
Sin hacer más comentarios
Somos novios, somos novios.
Siempre novios, somos novios.

Remembering what
  color the cherry trees are,
Without making any other comments.
We are sweethearts, we are sweethearts.
Always sweethearts, we are sweethearts.

Tres Palabras

Osvaldo Farres

Moderately

O ye la con-fe- sión,_____ de mi se-cre- to,_____ Na-ce de un co-ra-
zón_____ que es-ta de-sier- to;_____ Con tres pa-
la-bras te di - ré to-das mis co- sas,_____ Co-sas del co-ra-
zón_____ que son pre-cio- sas;_____ Da-me, tus man-os,
ven_____ to-ma las mí- as,_____ Que te voy a con-
fiar,_____ las an-sias mí- as_____ Son tres pa-
la-bras so - la - men-te mis an-gus- tias,_____ Y e-sas pa - la - bras son_____

1.
__ co - mo me gus - tas._____ O - ye la con-fe-

2.
gus - tas._____

Tres Palabras

Farres

Spanish Lyrics	English Translation
Oye la confesión	Listen to the confession
De mí secreto,	Of my secret,
Nace de un corazón	Born of a heart
Que esta desierto;	That is desolate;
Con tres palabras te diré	With three words that take
Todas mis cosas,	Everything of mine into account,
Cosas del corazón	Things of the heart
Que son preciosas;	That are precious;
Dame, tus manos, ven toma las mías.	Lady, take my hands in yours.
Que te voy a confiar	I'm going to entrust
Las ansias mías;	My worries to you;
Son tres palabras solamente	There are only three words
Mis angustias,	To my anguish,
Y esas palabras son	And the words are
¡Como me gustas!	I like you (a lot)!

Veracruz

Veracruz

A. Lara

Spanish Lyrics	English Translation

Yo nací con la luna de plata
Y nací con alma de pirata.
Yo he nacido rumbero y jarocho,
Trovador de veras;
Y me fui lejos de Veracruz.

I was born with the silvery moon
And born with a pirate's soul.
I'm the child of the rumba and the *jarocho*,
Country poet of the truth;
And I am far from Veracruz.

Veracruz, rincóncito donde hacen
Su nido las olas del mar.
Veracruz, pedacito de patria
Que sabe sufrir y cantar.

Veracruz, little corner where you have
Your nest in the waves of the sea.
Veracruz, little piece of the fatherland
That knows suffering and singing.

Veracruz, son tus noches diluvio
De estrellas , palmera y mujer.
Veracruz,
   vibra en mí ser.
Algún dia hasta tus playas
Lejanas tendré que volver.

Veracruz, where your nights are flooded
With the stars, palm trees, and women.
Veracruz, (you were meant to)
   vibrate with me.
Some day I want to
Return to your far-flung beaches.

Volver, Volver

Corrido Lento

F. Z. Mandonado

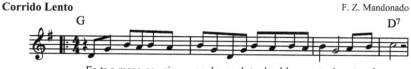

Es te_a mor a-pa - sio - na-do an-da to do_al-bo-ro - ta-do por vol - ver;

voy ca-mi-no_a la lo-cu-ra y_a un-que to - do me tor-tu - ra sé que-rer;

nos de-ja-mos ha-ce tiem-po pe-ro me lle-go_el mo-men-to de per - der.

Tú te - nías mu-cha ra-zón, le_ha - goca so_al co-ra - zón y me mue-ro por vol-ver.

y vol-ver, vol-ver, vol - ver   a tus bra-zos o - tra vez,

lle - ga-ré has - ta don-de_es - tés,   yo se per-der,   yo sé per-

der, quie-ro vol-ver, vol-ver, vol - ver.____

Volver, Volver   *Maldonado*

Spanish Lyrics	English Translation

Este amor apasionado   This passionate love
Anda todo alborotado por volver Is quickly returning.
Voy camino a la locura   I'm on my way to madness
Y aunqué toda me tortura,   And although everything tortures me,
sé querer.   I know how to love.

Nos dejamos hace tiempo   We left one another some time ago
Pero me llego el momento de perder   But the moment for me to lose has now come.
Tú tenias mucha razón   You were so right.
Le hago caso al corazón   I obey my heart
Y me muero por volver.   And I'm dying to come return.

Y volver, volver, volver,   And return, return, return,
A tus brazos otra vez,   To your arms once again,
Llegaré hasta donde estés   I will come to where you are
Yo sé perder, yo sé perder   I know how to lose, I know how to lose,
Quero volver, volver, volver.   I want to return, return, return.

Famous Mariachi Songs and Their Composers

La Adelita

This is one of the most popular selections of Mexican music. Its origin still remains somewhat of a mystery. The song is both tender and romantic but also contains an epic quality, which turned it into an igniting anthem during the revolutionary fever of 1910. Due to its popularity amongst the millions of oppressed peasants, as well as the men, women, and children who risked their lives on the battle field, *La Adelita* became the most popular song in the history of the Mexican Revolution.

Amor

The composer of this classic, Gabriel Ruiz, was known in the artistic environment of his times as "The Mexican Melody Maker." Ruiz was born in Guadalajara, the capital of the state of Jalisco. After his family moved to Mexico City when he was a youth, he was enrolled as a student at the National Conservatory of Music where he studied piano and composition. In 1935, he formed part of the cast of an important orchestra that regularly performed on Broadcasting Station XEW. Later, many of Ruiz's compositions were used in major productions of the Mexican theater, such as *Allende (The Brave)*.

This prolific artist prospered with his regular contributions to the Mexican Song Book. He was acknowledged as the master of the keyboard for more than a decade. His most noteworthy composition was definitely *Amor,* which was the first recorded song that featured him as a performer. It has since been recorded in virtually every country in the world by countless world music artists.

Aquellos Ojos Verdes

Aquellos Ojos Verdes is among the most delicate themes contained within any collection of romantic songs. It was written in the 1930s and is the inspired collaboration of Señores Nino Menedez and Adolfo Utrera. Adolfo, the lyricist, was madly in love with a girl to whom he dedicated his deeply felt words. He pleaded with Nino to set his lyrics to music, but, for the longest time, the latter refused. Finally, Menendez decided to compose a theme for his friend's love poem and that's how one of the most famous themes of all time was born. It's a timeless love ballad, whose success has crossed all international borders.

Besame Mucho

The composer of this classic, Consuelo Velázquez, was a native of Jalisco. At the tender age of four, she began to exhibit amazing musical abilities. She moved to Mexico City with her parents and soon began a long career as a concert pianist. The amazing fact was that she played solely "by ear," playing popular music that she arranged and interpreted.

She was frequently featured in the recitals at the prestigious Palace of Fine Arts. Her first major international hit came with her performance of her first original composition *Besame Mucho*. Velasquez's music has been recorded by Mexican musicians as well as by many in other countries. *Besame Mucho* has been translated into almost every language, sung by the best international artists, and performed by famous orchestras around the world.

141

Cielito Lindo

One of the most popular of Mexico's national songs is, without a doubt, *Cielito Lindo*. Although now in the public domain, the song was originally written by Quinine Mendoza.

Mendoza's fame grew with the advent of the radio and the phonograph. This particular standard exists in many different versions by musical artists worldwide, including several arrangements performed by Japanese orchestras.

El Rey

Here's an anecdote about this famous song's composer, maestro José Alfredo Jiminez, a native of Guanajuato. This story gives some insight into the posthumous success of *El Rey*.

Although this was one of the first songs that Jose Alfredo composed, he did not pursue its publication for many years after it was originally written, as he said, on many occasions, that the song "lacked consistency and it was just another theme." It appeared as though the song would stay unpublished, if not for the intervention of Lola Beltran, the "Queen of the *Rancheras*." She launched the first recording of the song, whose title later became Jiminez's nickname. For posterity, he will always be known as and identified with *El Rey*. Other songs written by this composer include *El Caballo Blanco, Ella, Paloma Negra, Serenita Huasteca* and *Si Nos Dejan*.

La Feria De Las Flores

One of the most beautiful and deeply felt songs in this collection is *La Feria De Las Flores,* written by the inspired Chucho Monge. The song reached its apex of popularity in the early 1940s. It was used as the musical theme for a movie of the same name released in 1942. Monge himself co-starred along with perhaps the greatest idol of the Mexican song, Pedro Infante. Another of Monge's compositions, *México Lindo* is also part of this collection.

Madrid

This song is only one of many classics written by perhaps the greatest Mexican composer of them all, Agustín Lara. Lara was born in Tlacotalpan, Veracruz, on October 30, 1900.

An interesting anecdote told by this very famous musician is that on the day he was born, the doctor who delivered him exclaimed to Lara's parents, "How ugly he is!" That description was to follow this brilliant composer throughout most of his life. On more than a few occasions, he described himself as ugly; he was probably described this way also because of his extreme slimness, as well as his homely facial characteristics. The Mexican music-loving public, however, soon elevated him to fame as the "skinny golden boy." He was a composer who first attained immortality with the publication of *Madrid*, a selection presented for the first time in 1945. It forms part of what is known as Lara's trilogy, The Spanish Rhapsody, *Granada, Madrid, y Veracruz,* all contained in this collection.

Sin Ti

The composer of this classic, Pepe Guizar, was born in Guadalajara, the capital of Jalisco. He wrote many beautiful songs which definitely captured the unique flavor of Mexico. He was praised as "The Musical Painter Of Mexico," as his songs were very colorful and evocative. In the 1940s he became one of his country's premiere radio personalities, accompanied by his group known as "The Foremen." In addition to this composition's lyric beauty, a romantic ballad acknowledged to be one of the most exquisite pages in the Mexican *mariachi's* repertoire, it also became the theme song for Los Panchos, the most popular *mariachi* trio of its time. Other songs written by this composer that are also represented in this collection are *El Mariachi* and *Guadalajara*.

Solamente Una Vez

Another classic written by Agustín Lara means that we will get to know more about this great composer, arguably the greatest in Mexican history. Lara, who attained international popularity with his songs, formed part of a Bohemian youth group that traveled to different cities in the state of Veracruz. He later emigrated to Mexico City. It is estimated that he completed more than a thousand songs in his much-heralded career, among them several that appear in this book—the aforementioned *Madrid* and the classics *Solamente Una Vez, Granada, Veracruz* and, in collaboration with his daughter Maria Teresa, *Noche De Ronda*.

Jurame

Maria Grever, the composer of this classic, was born on August 16, 1886, in Leon, Guanajuato. As a teenager, she was sent to France where she studied piano and composition with the world famous composer of *Claire de Lune,* Claude Debussy.

When Maria's father died, she returned to her parent's home in Mexico City, where she met and married a civil engineer, Leon Grever. They moved, shortly thereafter, to Jalapa, Veracruz. After some limited musical success there, she became disenchanted with her opportunities and was able to convince her husband to move to the United States where her musical talents blossomed. She originally performed as a concert pianist, interpreting the music written by the popular composers of the era. The drive to compose her own music soon overcame her desire to perform. Another song written by Grever that appears in this collection is *Cuando Vuelva a Tu Lado.*

(My thanks to Sergio Romano for this anecdotal information, compiled for a booklet of 150 popular songs widely distributed in Mexico by the Bimbo Baking Company.)

Selected Playlist

These are some of my favorite recordings of the songs included in this book. I hope that you will find your own favorites as you become more familiar with *mariachi* music.

Song	*Artist*	*Recording*
Amor	Gormé, Eydie	*Eydie Gormé & Trio Los Panchos*
Aquellos Ojos Verdes	Vargas, Pedro	*In Concert*
¡Ay, Jalisco No Te Rajes!	Mariachi Mexico	*Fiesta de Méxic*
Bésame Mucho	Miguel, Luis	*Romances*
Camino Real De Colima	Mariachi Vargas	*The Best Of Mariachi Vargas*
Chiapanecas	Faith, Percy	*Latin Rhythms*
Cielito Lindo	Montovani Orchestra	*In A Latin Mood*
Cocula	Beltran, Lola	*Tres Estrellas*
Cuando Calienta El Sol	Trio Los Panchos	*Los Panchos, Volumen 1*
Cuando Vuelva A Tu Lado	Cruz, Edgar	*Guitares de Amor*
Cucurrucucu Paloma	De Hoyos, Miguel	*Canciones de Amor*
De Colores	Orozco, Jose Luis	*Spanish Songs For Children*
Dos Arbolitos	Ronstadt, Linda	*Canciones de Mi Padre*
El Mariachi	Mariachi Mexico	*Fiesta de México*
El Rancho Grande	Guizar, Tito	*100 Classic Rancheras*
El Rey	Fernandez, Vicente	*Vicente Fernandez*
Ella	Infante, Pedro	*12 Grandes Exitos*
Gema	Cano, Nati	*Viva El Mariachi*
Granada	Carreras, Jose	*Great Songs*
Guadalajara	Fernandez, Vicente	*Lo Mejor de La Baraja con El Rey*
Guantanamera	Cruz, Edgar	*The Cruz Trio In Concert*
Inolvidable	Candido and Graciela	*Inolvidable*
Jarabe Tapatio	Mariachi Oro y Plata	*Jalisco, La Tierra Del Mariachi*
Jesusita	Mariachi Mexico	*100% Mariachi*
Jurame	Bocelli, Andrea	*Amore*
La Adelita	Negrete, Jorge	*La Adelita*
La Bamba	Mariachi Vargas	*The Best Of Mariachi Vargas*
La Cucaracha	Milva	*La Cucaracha*
La Feria De Las Flores	Mariachi Vargas	*The Best Of Mariachi Vargas*
Las Alteñitas	Pacheco, Miguel	*El Salterio*

146

Song	Artist	Recording
Las Mañanitas	Fernandez, Vicente	*Lo Mejor De La Baraja Con El Rey*
Llorarás, Llorarás	Mendoza, Amalia	*Serie Platino*
Madrid	Mariachi Vargas	*Mariachi Vargas De Tecalitlán*
Maria Elena	Mariachi Cobre	*Este Es Mi Mariachi*
México Lindo	Cano, Nati	*Llegarón Los Camperos*
Mi Ranchito	Nuñez, Estela	*100 Classic Rancheras*
No Volveré	Mendoza, Amalia	*La Tariacuri*
Noche De Ronda	Lara, Agustin	*Serie Platino: 20 Exitos*
Nunca, Nunca, Nunca	Bassey, Shirley	*Super Estrellas del Amor*
Ojos Españoles	Kaempfert, Burt	*Spanish Eyes*
Perfidia	Domingo, Placido	*De Mi Alma Latina*
Por un Amor	Reyes, Lucha	*100 Classic Rancheras*
Sabor a Mi	Santos and Jaramillo	*Sabor a Mi*
Siempre En Mi Corazón	Domingo, Placido	*Always In My Heart*
Sin Ti	Miguel, Luis	*Todos Los Romances*
Solamente Una Vez	Domingo, Placido	*De Mi Alma Latina*
Somos Novios	Manzanero, Armando	*El Piano*
Tres Palabras	Carr, Vikki	*Memories, Memorías*
Veracruz	Lara, Agustin	*Serie Platino: 20 Exitos*
Volver Volver	Fernandez, Vicente	*Vicente Fernandez*

Bibliography

Broughton, Simon and Ellingham, Mark. *World Music, The Rough Guide, Volume 2,* London, England: Rough Guides, Ltd., 2000

Benavidez, Rene. *Mariachi 101*, San Antonio, TX: International Folk Culture Center, 1996

Benavidez, Rene. *México, The Meeting of Two Cultures*, New York, NY: Higgins and Associates, 1991

Benavidez, Rene. *The History of Mariachi Music*, San Antonio, TX: International Folk Culture Center, 1996

Benavidez, Rene. *The Rhythm Instruments of The Mariachi Ensemble*, San Antonio, TX: International Folk Culture Center, 1996

Clark, Jonathan D. *The Latino Encyclopedia*, New York, NY: Marshall Cavendish Corp., 1996

Collins, Camille. *What is Mariachi?,* Jalisco, México: México Connect, 1996

Inclan, Roman. *Juan Gabriel: Survivor,* New York, NY: AARP *Segunda Juventud,* 2002

Olson, Dave A. and Sheehy, Daniel E. *Encyclopedia of World Music, Volume 2*, New York, NY: Garland Publishing, 1998

Perez, Leonor X. and Sobrino, Laura. *A History of Women in Mariachi,* Whittier, CA: *Mariachi* Publishing Company, 1998 & 2003

Sadie, Stanley and Tyrell, John. *The New Grove Dictionary of Music and Musicians,* New York, NY: Oxford University Press 2001

Toor, Frances. *Cancioneros Méxicano.* New York, NY: Bonanza Books, 1931

Toor, Frances. *A Treasury of Mexican Folkways*, New York, NY: Bonanza Books, 1937